koshad

The IEA Health and Welfare Unit

Choice in Welfare ¨ ⁀⁀

D1239354

From Welfare to Work:
Lessons from America

Lawrence M. Mead

Commentaries by
Dee Cook
Alistair Grimes
Eithne McLaughlin
Melanie Phillips
John Philpott

and

Frank Field MP
Minister for Welfare Reform

Edited by Alan Deacon

IEA Health and Welfare Unit
London

First published November 1997

The IEA Health and Welfare Unit
2 Lord North St
London SW1P 3LB

ISBN 0-255 36399-0
ISSN 1362-9565

Typeset by the IEA Health and Welfare Unit
in Bookman 10 point
Printed in Great Britain by
St Edmundsbury Press
Blenheim Industrial Park, Newmarket Road
Bury St Edmunds, Suffolk, IP33 3TU

Contents

Page

The Authors

Lawrence M. Mead is Professor of Politics at New York University, where he teaches public policy and American government. He has been a visiting professor at Harvard University, Princeton University, and the University of Wisconsin. He has also been a visiting fellow at Princeton and at the Hoover Institution at Stanford University.

Professor Mead is an expert on the problems of poverty and welfare in the United States, and the politics of these issues. He helped to develop the rationale for work requirements in welfare, and he is a leading scholar of how best to implement welfare/work programmes. He is currently researching welfare reform in Wisconsin.

He is the author of two widely-reviewed books, *Beyond Entitlement* (Free Press, 1986), a study of the work issue in federal social policy, and *The New Politics of Poverty* (Basic Books, 1992), and has edited *The New Paternalism* (Brookings Institution, forthcoming, 1997). He has also published many journal articles on welfare and employment, programme implementation, policy analysis, and public policy research, as well as more popular articles on 'workfare' and related issues.

Before going to NYU in 1979, Professor Mead held several policy and research positions in and around the federal government in Washington. He testifies regularly to Congress on poverty, welfare, and social policy.

He is a native of Huntington, New York, and a graduate of Amherst College. He received his Ph.D. in political science from Harvard University. During his postgraduate education he studied at Oxford University and held a Fulbright Scholarship at University College London.

Dee Cook is associate Dean of the School of Humanities and Social Sciences at the University of Wolverhampton. Her publications include: *Poverty, Crime and Punishment*, 1997; *Rich Law, Poor Law*, 1989; *The Wolverhampton Crime Audit*, 1996, with Martin Roberts; *Racism and Criminology*, 1993, edited with Barbara Hudson; *Paying for Crime*, 1989, edited with Pat Carlen. She has researched and published widely on issues around tax evasion; social security fraud; immigration and welfare policing;

racism, citizenship and exclusion; women on welfare; and crime
and locality.

Alan Deacon is Professor of Social Policy at the University of
Leeds. He edited the *Journal of Social Policy* between 1987 and
1991. He has written extensively on the history of social policy,
unemployment and the problems of single homeless people. His
books include *Reserved for the Poor*, with Jonathan Bradshaw,
1983 and *Roads to Resettlement*, with Jill Vincent and Robert
Walker, 1995. He was a member of the working party which
produced the *Report on Unemployment and the Future of Work* for
the Council of Churches of Britain and Ireland, 1997 and is the
author of *Benefit Sanctions for the Jobless: Tough Love or Rough
Treatment?*, Employment Policy Institute, 1997. He edited
Stakeholder Welfare for the IEA Health and Welfare Unit, 1996.

Frank Field MP was appointed Minister for Welfare Reform at
the Department of Social Security on 3 May 1997. As Deputy to
the Secretary of State, his responsibilities will also include an
overview of disability issues, work incentive and poverty matters,
responsibility for the Benefits Agency, and long-term planning.
Mr Field was elected to Parliament in 1979 as Member for
Birkenhead. He was Director of the Child Poverty Action Group
form 1969 to 1979, and of the Low Pay Unit from 1974 to 1980.
He was Opposition Front Bench Spokesman on Education
between 1980-81, and was Chairman of the Social Security
Select Committee from 1990. Mr Field was born in 1942 and
educated at St Clement Danes and the University of Hull. He is
the author of several publications on low pay, poverty and social
issues since 1971. He has taken particular interest in poverty
and income redistribution, and in ecclesiastical matters.

Alistair Grimes is currently the head of Sector Development for
Community Enterprise in Strathclyde. From 1988-1997 he was
Funding Controller with the Wise Group, developing its funding
base from £5 million to £14.5 million and bringing in £20 million
of European funds over that period. He has been involved in the
issues of poverty and employment since starting work with the
Scottish Council for Voluntary Organisations in 1979. He has
degrees in History from St Andrews, Politics from Durham and an
MBA and PhD from Edinburgh.

Eithne McLaughlin became Professor of Social Policy at the Queen's University of Belfast in 1995. She had previously held other academic posts at Queen's, the University of York and the University of Ulster, after some years in the voluntary sector. She was a member of the Commission on Social Justice, and has also served on The Standing Advisory Commission on Human Rights and The Eastern Health and Social Services Board in Northern Ireland. She has researched and published on unemployment, labour supply and social security issues, equality of opportunity, and informal and community care. She is currently Vice-Chair of the Social Policy Association and Vice-Chair of the Social Policy Committee of the Joint Universities Council for the Applied Social Sciences.

Melanie Phillips is a columnist for *The Observer* who writes about social issues and political culture. She is the author of *Divided House*, a study of women at Westminster, and co-author with Dr John Dawson of *Doctors' Dilemmas*, a primer on medical ethics. Her controversial book *All Must Have Prizes* (Little Brown) charts the disastrous effects of our culture of individualism upon the education system and the moral order.

John Philpott is an economist and has conducted research on labour market issues since completing his doctoral thesis at Oxford in the early 1980s. In 1987 he as appointed Director of the Employment Institute, an independent policy 'think tank', and in 1992, following the amalgamation of the Institute and Action Trust, he was appointed Director of the Employment Policy Institute (EPI). He has written widely on labour market issues and is a frequent contributor to media discussions on employment policy. He has acted as consultant to a number of national and international organisations including the Organis-ation for Economic Co-operation and Development (OECD), the International Labour Organisation and the United Nations. From 1993-1996 he was Specialist Adviser to the UK House of Com-mons Select Committee on Employment. He is author of *Working for Full Employment* (Routledge, 1996) and his report *A National Minimum Wage: Economic Effects and Practical Considerations* was published by the Institute of Personnel and Development in August 1996.

Foreword

This paper sets out an argument for requiring the recipients of public assistance to work in return for their benefits. I believe this is the most effective way to raise work levels among the needy. Many fewer adults work regularly among the poor than the better-off, and indeed lack of employment is the main reason people are poor today. In the United States, work requirements within welfare have shown more power to raise work levels among the poor than any other policy. Policy makers at the federal and state level have come around to this approach after voluntary programmes and efforts to improve opportunities did not suffice.

The meaning of 'workfare' is sometimes unclear. The term is often used in the United States to mean assigning welfare recipients to jobs in government or non-profit agencies where they receive no pay other than the aid they are already receiving. The term, however, can also mean any employment programme in which one must participate as a condition of aid. Such programmes may involve a range of activities—not only unpaid jobs but education or training or looking for work in the private sector. What makes these programmes 'workfare' is that they are mandatory, not that all clients must literally 'work off' their grants. This broader meaning is the more usual in the United States, and it is the one I will use below.

In several respects, the situation in the United States differs from that in Britain, and readers will want to keep these differences in mind. First, Americans seek to move mainly single mothers into work, since this is the group chiefly served by our means-tested aid programmes. Our principle cash assistance programme, now called Temporary Assistance for Needy Families (TANF), is akin to your Income Support, but it serves only families with children, chiefly headed by lone parents. Mandatory work programmes for this group are my main subject below. Other than Food Stamps, or coupons to buy food, we give very little means-tested aid to single people or men without families. We do have Unemployment Insurance, similar to your Unemployment Benefit, but its benefits usually last only six months. When they end, the jobless cannot usually transfer to means-tested aid as in Britain. So we count on the time limit to enforce work on this group, and unemployment benefits are not a focus of reform attention in the United States.

In Britain, in contrast, reform efforts focus on the unemployed much more than on dependent families. This is partly because you give more aid to men who fail to qualify for unemployment support or have exhausted it. In 1996, Unemployment Benefit and Income Support for the unemployed were merged in a Job-seeker's Allowance. The jobless who receive this are subject to increasing oversight, including 'Restart' interviews, to be sure they look for work. The new Labour government has proposed an ambitious youth employment scheme to be sure that more jobless young people enter jobs. Meanwhile, single mothers living on Income Support are subject to little direction to move them toward work. There is a Family Credit that subsidizes work for single mothers working at least 16 hours a week, but it is less generous than the American Earned Income Tax Credit, a similar wage subsidy that applies to all low-income workers. The Labour government has proposed new steps to bring more single parents into contact with employment centres, but these are far less forceful than the no-nonsense demands to work that are currently sweeping TANF in the United States.

A second difference between the countries is that American work programmes can assume a labour market that generates many available jobs. For us, a depression-like lack of work is a far lesser problem than the low wages that many of our jobs pay. It is thus feasible to require work, although it may also be necessary to subsidise the incomes of the poor even after they are working. In Continental Europe, jobs tend to be fewer but better-paying. Unemployment is higher, but the working popula-tion is seldom poor. The British situation appears to fall some-where between America and the Continent. British policy makers will have to ask how far your labour market permits work enforcement—and how far it may be necessary to create jobs.

Third, we have a long programme history and a great deal of research bearing on the difficulties of moving disadvantaged people into employment. Britain and Europe have less experience and research. So I do not assume that what works in America would necessarily transfer to the UK. British readers need to ask how parallel our conditions and traditions are to yours. Britain needs to do its own research and develop its own programmes. In that effort, however, you should find the American experience suggestive.

To describe the political controversy surrounding work programmes, I use the terms 'liberal' and 'conservative' in a different sense than they are used in the United Kingdom. They indicate not political parties but political tendencies. An American 'liberal' is someone who generally thinks public programmes can overcome social problems such as welfare dependency or poverty, and who thinks they should do so mainly by reforming society or giving benefits to needy people rather than trying to change their behaviour. A 'conservative' is someone who generally prefers private-sector rather than governmental solutions to problems and thinks the needy should be required to work or otherwise function in return for aid. In short, liberal social thinking is oriented to government and benefits, conservative thinking to the marketplace and good behaviour. Neither position is internally consistent, in that liberals seek 'community' but are reluctant to enforce community *mores*; conservatives do want to enforce values, but preferably through the marketplace rather than government.

In partisan terms, most American liberals are Democrats and most conservatives are Republicans. Neither creed nor party has the ideological associations that Labour or Conservative carry in Britain. Democrats are not socialists in the sense of the traditional Labour party, nor do Republicans have the traditionalist and pro-government aspects of the Conservative party. Rather, Democrats favour government interventions in the society for various worthy purposes, to promote racial or gender equality as well as economic fairness, while Republicans resist these as improper, costly or damaging to the economy. American Democrats are moralists and critics of social inequity rather than anti-capitalists, a direction toward which the Labour Party has recently shifted. The Republican vision is of a small-government, individualist society akin to what British Liberals promoted in the nineteenth century. The Democratic political base is among feminists, racial minorities, and intellectuals as well as trade unions, while Republicans draw upon cultural conservatives, including religious groups, as well as business and the better-off.

This paper is largely based on the following publications: Lawrence M. Mead, 'Raising Work Levels Among the Poor,' in *Reducing Poverty in America: Views and Approaches*, ed. Michael R. Darby (Thousand Oaks, CA: Sage Publications Inc., 1996), ch. 13; and Lawrence M. Mead, 'Welfare Employment,' in *The New Paternalism: Supervisory Approaches to Poverty*, ed. Lawrence M. Mead (Washington DC: Brookings, 1997), ch. 2. I gratefully acknowledge permission from these publishers to reprint parts of those papers here.

Lawrence M. Mead

Editor's Introduction:
Lawrence Mead and the
New Politics of Welfare

Alan Deacon

SPEAKING IN South Africa in October 1996 Tony Blair declared that a new Labour government would have 'failed' if it had not 'put in place at least the foundation stones of a modernised welfare state' at the end of its 'first five years'. The most pressing task, he argued, was to 'tackle the growing underclass in Britain today' which was characterised by 'long-term unemployment, welfare dependency, family instability, drug abuse,[and] poor educational opportunity and housing'.[1] In a later speech in Amsterdam he set out more fully the three principles upon which Labour would build a '21st Century Welfare State'. These were; a greater emphasis upon the responsibilities and obligations of claimants, a 'less dogmatic' approach to the balance between public and private provision, and a move towards provision which is 'active and not passive'.[2]

The new Prime Minister's commitment to welfare reform has been demonstrated repeatedly in the wake of Labour's election victory in May 1997. In the longer term his appointment of Frank Field as Minister for Welfare Reform may prove to be enormously significant. There is no question, however, that the dominant welfare issue in the first months of the new government, has been that of 'welfare to work' and that the key development has been the launch of Labour's 'New Deal' for the young unemployed.

The 'New Deal' offers young people who have been out of work for six months a choice between full time education, work in the private or voluntary sector, or a placement with an Environmental Task Force. What it does not offer them is the option of doing none of these things, and anyone who refuses to take part in the programme without good reason will be disqualified from benefit.[3] This degree of compulsion would have been unthinkable a few years ago, as would the statement by the new Chancellor, Gordon Brown, that the government's objective was not just to 'alleviate the problem of youth and long-term unemployment for a few months' but to develop a 'welfare state built around the work ethic'.[4]

New Labour's enthusiasm for 'welfare-to-work' schemes reflects a number of influences, including changes in economic ideas, the impact of communitarian thinking and a heightened sensitivity to the dangers of benefit fraud.[5] It is clear, however, that the form of the 'New Deal' owes much to Ministers' perceptions of developments in the United States, and particularly the increasing emphasis upon mandatory work requirements within welfare under first the Family Support Act of 1988 and latterly the Personal Responsibility and Work Opportunity Act of 1996.[6] It is equally clear that an important influence upon those developments has been the ideas and arguments of Lawrence Mead.

Lawrence Mead

Lawrence Mead is Professor of Politics at New York University. His first book, *Beyond Entitlement*, was published in the USA in late 1985, about a year after Charles Murray's *Losing Ground*. Like Murray, Mead began with an analysis of the apparent failure of the American War on Poverty. Like Murray, he believed that the growth in welfare dependency was due primarily to low work levels amongst the poor, and that this was not because jobs were unavailable, but because the poor either would not take them or could not keep them. Where Mead and Murray differed was in their assessment of the scope for welfare reform. In essence Murray claimed that the very existence of welfare made it easier for young women to become lone mothers and for young men to get by without a job or without accepting responsibility for their children. These 'perverse incentives' were inherent in welfare and the only effective remedy was to all but eliminate it: 'cut the knot for there is no way to untie it'.[7] In contrast, Mead argued that it was possible to make the administration of welfare more authoritarian, and to use it to enforce work and to demonstrate that 'willing work in available jobs is a defining obligation of the American polity'.[8]

The way to do this was, of course, to make eligibility for welfare conditional upon a demonstrated willingness to work. This rested upon an explicit assumption that the poor would find work if they looked for it and that, if necessary, they should be prepared to make their own arrangements for childcare in the same way as everyone else. This did not go unchallenged and Mead's debate with William Julius Wilson provides the clearest possible illustration of the differences between individualist and structuralist explanations of poverty and unemployment. During the course of that debate Mead did move towards an acceptance that it may be necessary for governments to introduce 'job enrichment measures' such as the provision of childcare. These, however, could be justified only after 'non-workers accept the jobs that exist. Only functioning citizens can claim new economic rights'.[9]

One of Mead's most striking arguments has been that the availability of jobs is not a technical issue, resolved by data, but a question of standards.

> If one defines acceptable jobs broadly but employability narrowly, as conservatives do, jobs will seem widely available. Equally if one sets more demanding standards for jobs but lower ones for workers, as liberals do, jobs will seem lacking.[10]

The real issue, then, was whether or not workers should adapt to the needs of the economy, and those who debated about jobs were 'really reasoning about permissible degrees of incompetency and dependency.' This theme was developed fully in Mead's second book, *The New Politics of Poverty*. Here Mead argued that the long-term workless poor are 'dutiful but defeated'. They want to work but lack the competence to do so on a regular basis. This means that there is simply no point in increasing the financial rewards for working. 'Incentives assume competence; the need is to create it'.[11]

Mead explains in this book how he believes that competence can be created through a combination of 'help and hassle', reinforced by sanctions for those who do not co-operate. The general significance of this argument must not be underestimated. Mead's criticism of those who assume competence on the part of the poor is a direct challenge to writers on both left and right who have highlighted the role of benefits in the creation of 'poverty traps' or 'unemployment traps'. Such an approach, he claims, 'has no solution to the passivity of today's poor, for their apparent inability to behave rationally even when opportunity exists'.[12] This is the crucial difference between him and Frank Field, as the latter makes clear in his commentary. Moreover, Mead has gone on to argue that the competence issue extends beyond the 'welfare-to-work' debate. The growing numbers of dysfunctional poor—of the underclass—has given rise to a new politics of poverty which is concerned not with the distribution of resources but with the breakdown of the family, crime and drug abuse. This new politics of conduct, he claims, is 'simply more salient than the politics of class'.

> The inequalities that stem from the workplace are now trivial in comparison to those stemming from family structure. What matters for success is less whether your father was rich or poor than whether you knew your father at all.[13]

The Commentaries

The main features of Mead's analysis are discussed in the six commentaries included in this book, and in his response to them. A key issue is the extent to which he is simply 'blaming the victim'. Back in 1986, Mead argued that roots of social disadvantage and exclusion were not to be found in inequitable social structures but in the failure of the poor to work. Welfare dependency itself, he wrote, 'undercuts the claims to equality' made on behalf of the poor. 'Those who only make claims can never be equal, in the nature of things, with those on whom the claims are made.' It follows, then, that the long-term consequences of compelling the poor to work is to lessen their isolation and alienation.

> Society must give up at least some of its fear of 'blaming the victim' if it is to help them more effectively. In part the choice it faces is whether to stigmatise the least co-operative of the disadvantaged in order to integrate the rest.[14]

This approach is diametrically opposed to the dominant academic tradition in British social policy, which holds that poverty and deprivation can only be understood in terms of social inequality. From this perspective, Mead's focus upon the behaviour of the poor is futile (because it is not addressing the cause of the problem) and unfair (because it is punishing people twice over for being born at the wrong end of a grossly unequal distribution of income and wealth). Dee Cook writes from this perspective and her essay reflects its fierce refusal to countenance what it sees as an outmoded individualism. Eithne McLaughlin also criticises Mead for 'victim blaming' and draws upon her previous work to argue that his assumptions about human motivation and decision-making are crude and simplistic.

A second set of issues concerns the lessons which can be learned from the operation of workfare in the United States. Would the authoritarian approach he favours work in the UK? Can compulsion be justified in principle? Can it be maintained in practice? John Philpott has in the past supported compulsion on the grounds that governments and unemployed have mutual or reciprocal obligations: the former to create worthwhile opportunities for work or training, the latter to make the most of those opportunities.[15] This is similar to the contractarian arguments put forward by ministers to justify the use of benefit sanctions within the 'New Deal'. Such arguments, however, place a greater emphasis than does Mead upon the quality of what is being offered to the unemployed, and particularly upon the provision of childcare or other forms of support.[16]

Alistair Grimes argues in defence of voluntary schemes, and cites the experience of the highly influential Wise Group to illustrate some of the likely consequences of introducing compulsion into such programmes. Both he and Philpott believe that the 'dutiful but defeated' constitute a relatively small proportion of the long term unemployed in the UK.

Finally, Melanie Phillips argues that the crucial difference between workfare in the USA and similar schemes in the UK is that the former is targeted primarily at lone mothers. What, she asks, is the basis for assuming that paid work is always appropriate for these women? Why is so little attention paid to the effects on the children? Workfare, she argues, may be a solution to the problem of welfare dependency, but it does not solve the broad problems which arise from the disintegration of the family. Frank Field, however, is clear that the UK has much to learn from the experience of case-management in the USA, and especially in Wisconsin.

The commentators write from different perspectives. All are critical of Mead's position to some degree. All, however, are agreed about the importance of the 'welfare-to-work' debate and of Lawrence Mead's contribution to it.

From Welfare to Work: Lessons from America

Lawrence M. Mead

Glossary

AFDC	Aid to Families with Dependent Children
CETA	Comprehensive Employment and Training Act
EITC	Earned Income Tax Credit
FAP	Family Assistance Plan
FSA	Family Support Act of 1988
GAIN	Greater Avenues for Independence
HCD	Human Capital Development
JOBS	Job Opportunities and Basic Skills Training Program
LFA	Labor Force Attachment
MDRC	Manpower Demonstration Research Corporation
PBJI	Program for Better Jobs and Income
PRWORA	Personal Responsibility and Work Opportunity Reconciliation Act of 1996
SWIM	Saturation Work Initiative Model
TANF	Temporary Assistance for Needy Families
WIN	Work Incentive Program

1

Poverty and the Failure to Work

THIS ESSAY attempts, with a broad brush, to describe the problem of low work levels among poor adults, assess the usual explanations for it, and suggest the best approach to solving it, which I believe is work requirements within the welfare system. Few poor adults work regularly. That is the main reason they are poor, and it is difficult to trace the problem to limitations of opportunity, such as low wages or lack of jobs. Programmes that try to supplement wages for the low-skilled or to raise their skills may be worthwhile, but they neglect the greater need, which is simply to cause poor adults to put in more hours at the jobs they can already get. Voluntary programmes or other opportunity measures do not achieve this.

To raise work levels, an effort to enforce work is unavoidable. Work requirements in welfare show promise. By 'welfare' here I chiefly mean Temporary Assistance for Needy Families (TANF), the national assistance programme, mainly for single-parent families, that is run with both federal and state money. Created in 1996, TANF is a renamed and restructured version of Aid to Families with Dependent Children (AFDC). The new law contains the toughest work-tests yet enacted. The work approach is more realistic than radical-sounding proposals to end or transform welfare. It is also, however, deeply controversial. Dispute over what can be expected of poor people, not lack of opportunity, is the main reason chronic poverty persists in America.[1]

Poor persons are highly diverse, as are the causes of poverty. I will not discuss children or elderly people who are poor, although their problems are important. My analysis applies mainly to working-age adults, who are the most controversial of the poor population and the key to any solution to poverty. I also concentrate mainly on long-term poor adults, meaning those who are poor for more than two years at a stretch, because they are the hardest to help and the most important politically. This is the group that most exercises the public and is most debated among experts. In the urban setting, these poor people primarily mean long-term welfare mothers and low-skilled single men, who are often the absent fathers of welfare families. These long-term, employable, poor adults are not a large group—perhaps five per cent of the population[2]—but they are at the core of the poverty problem.

Why Work Must Be Enforced

The idea that the poor must be *required* to work, not just offered the chance to, has emerged in American social policy because of the nature of the poverty problem and our failure to solve it on a voluntary basis.

The Employment Problem

Overwhelmingly, today's working-age poor are needy, at least in the first instance, because the adults in these families do not work normal hours. American society assumes that families will be supported mainly by parents' earnings. Table 1 (p. 52) shows that more than three quarters of the heads of American families were employed in 1995, and well over half worked full-year and full-time. Even among single mothers, who have child-rearing responsibilities, the work level was two-thirds. For heads of households generally, work levels have fallen slightly since 1959, but among female heads they have risen, reflecting the movement of women into the labour force. Other data show that families with children have increased their work effort since 1970,[3] in their oft-noted struggle to keep up with inflation.

But as Table 2 (p. 52) shows, work levels among poor people are dramatically lower and have fallen much more sharply. In 1959, two-thirds of the heads of poor families worked, and nearly a third worked full-year and full-time. Those figures fell to half and 16 per cent respectively during the 1970s and 1980s, before rising a bit in the 1990s. Work levels among poor welfare recipients are also low, with only eight per cent of welfare mothers reporting employment in a given month, even part-time.[4] For the moment, I say nothing about causes.

There is some evidence that poor adults work more than they report. Poor families appear to spend more income than they say they receive. Half or more of welfare recipients may work over time, often without reporting the income to avoid reductions in their grants. Some experts conclude from this that most poor who seem not to work are actually employed. They simply do not acknowledge it to keep welfare support or because their jobs are in the underground economy. In this view, the cause of poverty is not low work-effort but low wages that do not allow mothers to live on their earnings or to combine work and welfare legally.[5] Such conclusions go too far. Welfare mothers are needy mainly because of low working hours, not low wages. Unreported work is seldom sustained and is uncommon among long-term dependent persons.[6] Work levels among single mothers on welfare are clearly much lower than among single mothers not on welfare, among whom the work rate is about 85 per cent.[7]

Much of the decline in work levels, it is true, reflects the decline in the poverty level since 1959. As real wages rose, most working poor people earned their way out of poverty. It is now difficult to work normal hours and remain poor, so almost by definition the remaining poor are mostly people without jobs. But there clearly is a work decline even allowing for this. If poverty were defined relative to average incomes, rather than in absolute terms as it is by the government's poverty measure, then the poverty line would rise with economic growth, and there would be more working poor. Let us define the poor as the bottom fifth of the family income distribution. There now is no clear work decline after 1970 for poor families in general, but there still is for families with children, whose poverty is the most critical. These low-income families worked less, just when better-off families were working more.[8]

The decline is not because of a fall in the share of poor persons who are of working age. It is often thought that needy people are largely made up of children or older persons. Actually, the proportion of poor who are working-aged (ages 18 to 64) rose from 42 per cent to 51 per cent between 1959 and 1995.[9] The reasons for this include a decline in the number of children per family and the drop in poverty among retired persons because of rising social security payments. Rather, the decline in work is linked to the growth in female-headed families, mostly at the lowest income levels. Poor female heads themselves are not working less—as Table 2 (p. 52) shows, their work level has always been low. But now more such families are among the poor, and this reduces the work level for the poverty population as a whole.

Work effort by female heads in general is rising. Poor female heads, however, work less than others, and poor adults seem to be working less whether or not they are married. Among blacks, who compose most of the long-term poor population, two thirds of poor female-headed families were needy before the breakup of the parents as well as after, equally because of non-work.[10] As Table 2 (p. 52) shows, even among the heads of poor married-couple families, a sizable work decline has occurred. Some of this reflects greater retirement among older persons and persons who are disabled. But even if one defines the employable stringently, excluding persons who are older and disabled, students, and parents with children under six, since 1967 the share of poor family heads who could work has risen while the share actually working has fallen.[11]

Table 3 (p. 53) compares work levels among the general population and the poor population for individuals and for several groupings of family heads in 1995. In all categories, the difference is enormous. Employment is 20 or 30 percentage points higher for the general population than among poor people. Most significant, the multiple for full-year, full-time work is three or four times higher. It is lack of steady work, not lack of all employment, that mostly separates poor adults from non-poor adults. If one compares poor persons with non-poor persons, rather than with the overall population, as in Table 4 (p. 53, data for 1991), the contrasts are even greater.

These differences directly account for most of today's poverty. Table 5 (p. 54) shows how poverty rates vary with work level for the same demographic groups as in Table 3. The effect of employment is tremendous. Non-workers suffer poverty at as much as five times the rate occurring among workers. Nearly 80 per cent of female family heads with children are poor if they do not work; only 13 per cent—about average for the population—are poor if they work full-year and full-time. Work has the same potent effect on dependency. Two thirds of female family heads are on welfare among those who do not work, whereas only seven per cent are on welfare among those who work full-year and full-time.[12]

Of course, other factors than work-effort determine whether people are poor. Non-workers more often have to care for children than workers do, and they would average lower earnings than those currently employed if they took a job. If they worked steadily, more would remain poor even with employment than is true of existing workers. If one allowed for these factors, poverty levels would not vary so extremely with work level as in Table 5. Nevertheless, the effect of non-work is so great that overcoming it is strategic for reducing poverty. And, as discussed below, if work levels among poor people were to recover to former levels, providing aid to poor people would also be more popular.

Non-work is costly for poor families in other than income terms. It contributes to the problems of lifestyle that, as much as low income, conspire to keep people needy today. It is often said that the problems of poor people are rooted in the family, particularly the absence of fathers. But the greatest reason why poor adults fail as parents is inability to function as breadwinners. Fathers leave families mainly because they do not work steadily. One of the reasons poor children often fail in school and later on the job is that they have not had the example of parents working consistently outside the home.

2

What Stops the Poor from Working?

THE WORK problem is so important that, in large part, the debate about poverty is a debate about employment. The great question is why poor adults work so much less consistently than better-off adults. The tradition among experts has been to seek impediments outside poor people themselves. Perhaps low wages leave people poor even if they work or discourage them from working. Perhaps poor people are barred from employment by sheer lack of jobs or childcare, racial bias, or the disincentives set up by the welfare system, which reduces a family's grant in proportion to earnings. Perhaps they simply cannot work because of the burdens of childrearing, disability, or a lack of marketable skills.

All these theories have drawn intense research attention. In my opinion, that effort has not come up with much. Each of the theories appears to be a little bit true, but none of them—singly or in combination—appears to explain more than a small part of the work problem.[1]

The trouble with the wage theory is that if most poor adults are not even employed, low wages cannot cause their poverty. If 'working poverty' were more prevalent, this theory would be more persuasive. It is true that 61 per cent of poor families reported earnings by some family member during 1995, but poor families with year-round, full-time workers were still greatly outnumbered by those with no workers—1.8 million to 2.9 million.[2] It is commonly said that work does not pay low-skilled individuals enough to be worthwhile. But it clearly pays them enough to avoid poverty and welfare in most cases, provided the adults in families work the hours typical of society. That means full-year and full-time for the family head, with at least some work by the spouse or another family member.

Poverty is often blamed on the minimum wage because it is assumed that when poor adults go to work, this is what they earn. It is easy to show that working even full-year and full-time at the minimum wage cannot support a family above poverty. But such calculations mean little because the vast majority of poor workers actually earn above the minimum wage; they are poor mainly because of low working hours. Few minimum-wage workers have to try to support a family alone. Most are secondary workers, usually spouses or teenage children, in families in which the head is working for more than the minimum wage. For these reasons, the minimum wage actually has little connection to poverty. In 1985, only 19 per cent of minimum-wage workers were poor, whereas only 26 per cent of poor workers earned at or below the minimum wage.[3] Congress has raised the minimum wage twice since then—most recently to $5.15—and this has reduced the link between it and poverty still further.

Poverty also has little connection to low wages in general. As Table 5 (p. 54) suggests, few steady workers at any wage are poor. Even low-wage workers today are seldom poor, and they are even more seldom heads of poor families.[4] Again, low working hours are a more important cause of poverty than low wages. One might suppose that low wages barred work for single mothers, who must stay on welfare because they cannot support their families and pay for childcare on one income. Most welfare spells are short, however, and most of them end through employment,[5] so wages must usually be adequate to work off the rolls. By one estimate, if one allows for child support and childcare costs as well as wages, half or more of welfare mothers could escape dependency if they worked full-time.[6] The great majority of single mothers who avoid poverty do work full-time or have working family members.[7] It is valid to say that mothers cannot work off welfare without higher wages only if we accept their current low hours as given.

To contend that low wages or benefits are central to poverty, one would have to show that they were a cause of low working hours as well as low returns per hour. Perhaps low wages and benefits discourage low-skilled people from working, whereas higher returns would cause them to put in more hours. Research has not shown, however, that work effort among the poor responds much to this sort of incentive. The labour supply of low-income workers is remarkably unresponsive to payoff levels.[8] Employment by welfare mothers is little affected by welfare benefit levels or by the wages the mothers are able to earn.[9] It is work effort by the middle class that has responded to stagnant wages in recent decades—and by rising, not falling.

Other theories of non-work also have small support. There is some evidence that employers discriminate against minorities in favour of whites, if one controls for all factors except race.[10] But all factors usually are not equal. Urban businesses typically have found unskilled black workers, especially men, to be unreliable employees. It is mainly this, rather than bias aimed at skin colour, that now makes many employers—including blacks —reluctant to hire from the inner city. The opposition is based on experience and does not, like traditional bias, hold non-white groups to be inferior in general. There may be some 'statistical' discrimination, in that some individuals who would be good employees are not hired because their racial group has a bad reputation. But the extent is probably limited because employers use a number of indicators—class and job history as well as race—to pick among job applicants.[11]

Welfare disincentives to work are surprisingly unimportant. Research finds that work levels on welfare are low across the nation regardless of the level of welfare benefits.[12] A related theory is that welfare recipients are deterred from working by fear of losing health coverage. They get Medicaid while on welfare, whereas many low-wage jobs lack health insurance. In fact, this effect seems confined to the families with the worst health problems and is not a major cause of dependency or non-work.[13]

The presence of pre-school children does not appear to deter welfare mothers from working; numbers of children do deter, but the importance of this has fallen with the size of welfare families, which today mostly include only one or two children. Childcare seldom appears to be a serious barrier to employment because it is much cheaper and more available than advocates assert. In 1988 only nine per cent of childcare arrangements relied on institutional facilities such as childcare centres, and most mothers paid nothing at all for care. The situation is similar among welfare mothers.[14]

The most widely discussed barrier to opportunity for those who are poor is an alleged lack of all employment in inner-city areas. Research has shown, however, that jobless poor people seldom face a situation like the Depression. Groups with high unemployment, such as minorities, women, and youth, are characterised more by rapid job turnover than long-term joblessness.[15] Such individuals usually say they can find jobs, but they also leave them quickly. The reasons include children at home, conflict with superiors and co-workers, and the low-paid, unattractive character of available jobs.

Of course, jobs are less available during a recession but people who keep looking for work usually find it. The problem in the ghetto is more that many people are out of the labour force entirely. Even when the urban labour market is tight enough to lower unemployment sharply, this does not significantly increase the proportion of disadvantaged persons who seek to work.[16] At present, economists agree, jobs at some legal wage appear to be widely available in cities, at least to those seeking them at a given time. The continuing influx of foreign immigrants, both legal and illegal, into the US is just one proof of this. Possibly, the number of jobs would be insufficient if all the non-workers sought positions at once, but a literal job shortage is not now a major cause of poverty. A far more serious limitation is the low wages paid by most of the available positions.[17]

Economic Trends

The theory that jobs are lacking rests heavily on the notion that the economy today offers much less opportunity to poor persons than it once did. In the last two decades, the decline of manufacturing has idled many workers, real wages have grown little, and inequality among incomes has risen. Less educated workers, especially among younger men, have suffered actual losses in earnings. All this, it is said, is the major cause of today's non-work and poverty. It seems obvious that the destruction of millions of manufacturing jobs in American cities since the 1970s must have radically reduced the opportunities available to today's low-skilled job seekers.[18]

Popular accounts of the trends, however, typically do not allow for the vast expansion of employment in service industries in the 1970s and 1980s or for the recent drop in the number of new entrants to the labour force because of the fall of birth rates following the 'baby boom'. These trends gradually tightened the labour market in the last decade, despite the decline of factory jobs. As a result, immigrants from all over the world continued to flock to the US. Not only do they find jobs, but so many jobs are available there is little evidence that the newcomers have reduced job availability for the native-born.[19] One recent study finds that the combination of immigration and imports might explain up to half of the decline of wages for school drop-outs relative to wages for other workers.[20] But this still does not explain the main mystery—why the low-skilled increasingly fail to work at all.

The theory that de-industrialisation is responsible for the disorders of the ghetto has limited support. Although manufacturing jobs clearly are fleeing the inner city, this may be the result and not the cause of social disorders there.[21] And because population is leaving the older cities faster than jobs, the labour market may actually be tightening in urban centres. Although more jobs are available in the suburbs than the cities, openings apparently remain accessible to most people seeking them, wherever they live. Studies that attempt to tie the employment of urban dwellers to the proximity of jobs report weak findings at best. The idea of a spatial mismatch may be partially valid in the most depressed cities of the East and Midwest but probably not in the most prosperous South or West.[22] Some analysts talk instead of a skills mismatch, with the poor lacking the talent to get work in an increasingly high-tech economy because of weak education. Most jobs, however, still demand only low or moderate skills. Urban employers complain mostly about employees' lack of basic work discipline—inability to show up for work and take orders—rather than a lack of advanced skills.

Non-work is a cause of growing inequality in that the decline of work habits of those at poverty levels is one reason why wages and earnings for the low-skilled have fallen.[23] But it is hard to argue the other way, that economic trends explain why few poor people work regularly. Certainly, economic change has caused hardships, but the impact has been mainly on factory workers with a steady employment history, few of whom are needy. Few poor or homeless men held good jobs before falling into destitution.[24] Unquestionably, manufacturing workers face a struggle to preserve their livelihoods, but that battle is going on largely over the heads of the poor population.

The last two recessions, it is true, were especially severe, and this has unnerved the public. The downturn of the early 1980s abruptly cut well-paid blue-collar employment. Since the recession of 1990-1991, many other industries have been downsizing, producing unprecedented unemployment among white-collar workers. This has led some to fear that the jobs bonanza is over and that long-term unemployment is due to rise. Concern over jobs was a major factor in President Clinton's initial election in 1992.

But these fears always dissipate as the economy recovers. Most displaced factory workers found other jobs quickly. Current white-collar jobless persons are likely to do so more easily. Fears that economic change would render any large part of the workforce obsolete have never proved valid in the past and are unlikely to in the future. Since growth resumed in 1991, job creation has been prodigious, with many new positions created at both high and low wages. Even the manufacturing sector has recovered. The restructuring of the economy is likely to lead in time to larger gains in productivity and higher real wages.[25] In the late 1980s, the proportion of the adult population employed reached 63 per cent, the highest figure ever. The last recession cut that to all of 62 per cent.[26] A serious employment problem remains highly improbable.

In any event, the work attachment of long-term poor persons is too limited today for their predicament to have much connection to the vicissitudes of the economy. The problems of the ghetto, including non-work, are much the same in good times and bad. There are still some working poor people, so the overall levels of poverty and the welfare rolls do rise and fall with economic growth. But we should not conclude that the bulk of poverty or dependency has economic causes. Since 1980, the poverty rate has varied only between 13 per cent and 15 per cent across two sharp recessions followed by two lengthy booms. Although a strong economy still helps to lower poverty, the gains will be marginal as long as work levels remain low.

I do not mean that the barriers are unimportant. My judgement is that about a third of the work problem among the seriously poor might be attributable to limits to opportunity in all forms, the extent varying around the country. Differences in opportunity have a great deal to do with who gets ahead in America. Differences in education, especially, heavily determine who gets a good job and who gets a lesser one. Although bias unrelated to conduct appears to be a minor problem for poor persons, it is probably a larger problem for employed minorities, who face white resistance to their assuming positions of authority in government and the private sector.

But in general, social structure appears to have more influence on employed persons than on jobless poor persons. It is largely *after* people go to work that they encounter barriers, not before. Impediments have a lot to do with *inequality among workers*. They have little to do with *failure to work at all*, which is the greater problem for today's needy.

The Culture of Poverty

More important than any economic factor as a cause of poverty, I believe, is what used to be called the culture of poverty. Surveys and ethnographic studies suggest that poor adults want to work and observe other mainstream values. Many, however, resist taking the low-paid jobs that are most likely to be available to them. A greater number are simply defeatist about work or unable to organise their personal lives to hold jobs consistently. These feelings are rooted, in turn, in the historic lack of opportunity that minority groups—who compose most of the poor—knew in this country and in their countries of origin in the past. Of course, most members of these groups are employed and not poor. But some remain unconvinced that it is worth striving in America, despite the equal opportunity reforms of recent decades. This element has given rise to much of the underclass.

Equally important is that values such as the need to work are no longer well enforced in ghetto areas. The middle class, which upheld these *mores*, has largely moved out, and public institutions have failed to fill the gap. In large measure, non-work results simply because welfare and other public programmes do not yet require most adult recipients to work as a condition of support. Similarly, crime results from weak law enforcement, and illiteracy results from the decline of standards in the schools. The loss of authority by these institutions has more to do with poverty than any recent changes in the economy or society.[27]

The Limits of Opportunity

Policies to expand opportunity for the disadvantaged on a voluntary basis can make only a limited contribution to overcoming poverty. Such policies presume that the cause of non-work lies in some impersonal constraint. Today's long-term poverty, however, is seldom visited on people by nameless social forces. It is rarely the result of steady workers being shut out of jobs or paid starvation wages. Poverty of this structural type was much more prevalent before 1960 than since. Rather, need usually results in the first instance from self-defeating actions by poor people themselves, particularly non-work, unwed childbearing, and crime.

The tradition has been to assume that this behavioural poverty, like the structural type, would respond to enhancements of opportunity. Give those who are poor a better chance to make it, and they will behave more constructively. Expanded opportunity, through a combination of the private sector and government largesse, certainly has been at the heart of the American dream for most people. Liberals want to offer the same chances to poor people by inventing new social programmes. Conservatives want to do it through greater reliance on the private sector. Both sides assume that some change in social arrangements can liberate those who are needy to get ahead.

Both approaches, however, make what I call the competence assumption. They presume that the individuals to be helped have the capacity at least to advance their own self-interest, if not society's. Particularly, people will seize the chance to get ahead economically by getting an education and then working hard in the best job they can get. That is the presumption that has proven invalid for many of today's poor people. Too often, they do not get through school or work consistently. Dysfunction has defeated the preferred opportunity approaches of both left and right. Big government during the Great Society era (the 1960s and 1970s) achieved some good things, as did smaller government under Reagan and Bush (the 1980s and early 1990s). But neither approach could eradicate entrenched poverty, in both cases mainly because of the work problem. Neither more government nor less can overcome need as long as poor adults do not reliably take jobs.

My sense is that the opportunity structure has little influence on personal behaviour in the present. Social arrangements affect how people are rewarded if they function but not whether they function. Rather, the ability to cope stems largely from one's family and upbringing. Children are formed in the family, and once they leave it there is remarkably little government can do to change them or to enhance their capacities. At best, it can restrain the behaviour of people who cope poorly, who otherwise would injure themselves and their children, in hopes that the children will function better.

Poverty would be easy to solve if only resources, and not governance, were required. Both left and right naturally search for some way to 'invest' that would overcome the social problem without addressing conduct. For liberals, that means spending more on poor families through welfare or intensive service programmes.[28] For conservatives, it might mean special education programmes to build up skills, job placement programmes, or job creation in the private sector. But the effect of even the best of such efforts is limited and long-term. It would be better to invest in high-quality social administration because bureaucracy—unpopular though it is—increasingly must manage the lives of those who are seriously poor.

Functioning ability does connect to opportunity, but chiefly well back in time. The root of most of today's serious poverty probably is in the historic denials of opportunity for blacks and other minority groups, who today make up a majority of those who are poor. For blacks, the trouble goes back to the decades of unequal opportunity that followed the emancipation of blacks in the Civil War. Black society was actually more coherent under Jim Crow than it is today. But the lack of a fair chance for black men to 'make it' in the industrial economy took its toll. The majority of blacks kept faith, prepared themselves, and when civil rights came, were ready to advance into the working and middle classes. The others lost faith in America and themselves. The disillusionment of poor blacks and, later, Hispanics caused the ghettoes to crumble just when the doors of opportunity opened.[29]

These memories now prevent improved opportunity from solving the social problem. Today's seriously poor people typically do not believe that they will ever have a chance to make it, although black success is now commonplace and discrimination in the old sense is rare. And because their problems are perpetuated by weak families, no further reforms by government are likely to convince them otherwise. They project their hopelessness onto the environment, but the feeling really arises in the first instance from weak or abusive parenting. No improvement in the wider setting can make them hopeful, because none can undo those early experiences. Their despair has become immune to social change.

The solution lies in rebuilding the family, not society. Most children acquire a sense of possibility not because society is fair to them but because adults near to them are. By identifying with parents and teachers, they internalise values. By meeting their expectations, they also derive a sense of mastery that makes them approach life hopefully, without defeating themselves. The wider world has no comparable influence. If parents are effective, children will be well formed even if the surrounding society is unfair. Exemplary black figures such as Martin Luther King and Marian Wright Edelman were the products of an unjust society but also of strong families that upheld demanding standards for them.[30] Conversely today, family breakdown has undercut functioning even though society has become much more fair. The main task of social policy is no longer to reform society but to restore the authority of parents and other mentors who shape citizens.

Government has no easy way to do that, but the best single thing it can do is to restore order in the inner city. Above all, it can require that poor parents work, because employment failures are the greatest cause of family failures. If parents do not work, no programme to help the children is likely to achieve much. To a child, to have functioning parents is worth 25 Head Start programmes. Only if parents work and fulfill other civilities, such as obeying the law, can they have the self-respect needed to command the respect of their children.

Those who would be free must first be bound. Parents who would bequeath freedom to their children must first live orderly lives. The source of bondage for today's seriously poor is no longer social injustice but the disorders of their private lives. For these Americans, the way forward is no longer liberation but obligation.

3

Making Work Pay

IN LIGHT of this analysis, I do not believe that further efforts to improve opportunities for the poor population can overcome poverty, although they can make some contribution.[1] The current vogue is to try to 'make work pay'. The first Clinton administration took steps to raise the returns of low-skilled jobs. But if poverty is mostly the result of low working hours rather than low wages, then improving the rewards of work can have only a marginal effect.

Congress raised the minimum wage to $5.15 in 1996. It might raise it again, but most of the benefit would go to non-poor persons, simply because most minimum-wage workers are already above poverty. Without more poor people working at or near the minimum, raising the floor is no longer an effective anti-poverty strategy.[2] One could also increase the Earned Income Tax Credit (EITC), a subsidy for low-income workers with children. Because the EITC directly targets poor workers, it is the most efficient means of helping them. Congress raised the EITC substantially in 1990 and 1993. In 1996, the credit paid a low-income worker 34 per cent of the first $6,330 in earnings ($2,152) if the family had one child and 40 per cent of the first $8,890 ($3,560) if there were two or more children.[3] Even if the EITC is generous, however, it cannot reach most poor families simply because few poor adults are employed.

Neither measure is likely to raise working hours. In fact, increases may depress hours. A higher minimum wage probably reduces work levels because it eliminates some jobs, and this causes some youths to withdraw from the labour force. A higher minimum wage and a higher EITC also reduce work effort because low-wage workers who qualify can now make the same income with fewer working hours. This motivation is apparently stronger than the incentive to work more hours that is generated

16

by raising the returns per hour; in the terms economists use, the income effect dominates the substitution effect. Although these reductions are probably small,[4] they do suggest that 'making work pay' can be counterproductive as long as work levels remain low.

Another approach is to try to weaken the disincentives in welfare that many believe deter the dependent from working. Liberals try to do this by raising work incentives, that is, by limiting the reductions in welfare benefits when welfare recipients have earnings. Conservatives prefer to do it simply by reducing the number of employed or employable people who can get on welfare in the first place. The trouble is that neither strategy has shown much effect on work levels. The work incentives that existed in AFDC between 1967 and 1981 did not palpably raise work effort among recipients, and the Reagan cuts in these incentives in 1981 did not reduce effort.[5]

None of this is to say that higher wages, benefits, or work incentives are not warranted on other grounds. Government may decide that it should ensure workers a living wage or health care or other advantages as an act of justice. Society is entitled to define and redefine the package of rewards and obligations that constitute citizenship in America.[6] My point is only that improving the package connected to work can do little to overcome poverty as long as few of the poor are steady workers.

The other popular approach to raising earnings has been voluntary education and training programmes. For 30 years Washington has financed a succession of 'compensatory' programmes designed to improve the skills of poor persons so that they could get 'better' jobs. The evaluations of these programmes show that typically they are efficient rather than effective. They raise the earnings of their clients by enough to justify their costs, but the gains are small, not enough to solve the work or poverty problem. The largest increases have been for women, not for men, and most of them have come from causing the clients to work more steadily in jobs they could already get, not from getting them better jobs. It is not surprising that disadvantaged clients find it difficult to learn greater skills because they have usually done poorly in school and are often dropouts.[7]

Making Jobs

A more controversial strategy is public employment. If one believes that jobs, or 'good' jobs, are lacking for poor persons, government ought to create them. But this strategy was tried in the 1970s, a troubled decade in which jobs were much more plausibly lacking than they are today. Under the Comprehensive Employment and Training Act (CETA), Washington funded up to 750,000 positions a year in local government and non-profit agencies. The programme was costly, gains in earnings were marginal at best, and after CETA most clients did not go on to employment in the private sector. Even liberals abandoned the programme, and it was abolished by Ronald Reagan. If it were revived, it would hardly change the conviction many poor people have in cities that work is impossible for them.

Voluntary approaches tend to assume a solution to the work problem rather than providing it. They all presume that the poor are primed to work and only require a better chance to get ahead. They seek to guarantee, in Ellwood's phrase, that 'If you work you shouldn't be poor'.[8] But satisfying that *if* turns out to be most of the problem. For if poor persons worked regularly, they would usually not be poor for long in the first place. Voluntary programmes tend to reach mainly the transiently poor, the families that already have a work history or working members. They tend not to reach the more disadvantaged welfare recipients and single men, who are much more central to entrenched poverty.

Voluntary programmes can play a role in a solution. I do not oppose them out of hand, although costs must be considered. But we must recognise that they do not reach to the core of the work problem, which is the reluctance of poor adults to take and hold the low-skilled jobs they can already get. To 'make it,' these Americans have to display something more like the tenacity in seeking and retaining work that immigrants to this country often do. Without that change in behaviour, endless additional training and service programmes can be tried and can 'succeed' without seriously denting the social problem.

4

Radical Solutions from Right and Left

ONE RESPONSE to these disappointments has been to say that the voluntary measures tried to date do not change the existing system enough. Do something more radical to change the programme structure or the environment, and then work levels will rise. But arguments to this effect—from the right as well as the left—are unconvincing.

Some conservative experts say that federal welfare programmes should simply be abolished. Without public support for female headed families, this argument goes, poor adults could not get away with producing children without supporting them—the central cause of poverty. They would have to marry and go to work, and the disorders of the ghetto would recede. Giving aid sounds humane but inevitably promotes dysfunctional behaviour. Denying aid sounds severe but promotes self-reliance and, thus, is the only true way to help poor people.[1]

The recent welfare reform tends in this direction. The Personal Responsibility and Work Opportunity Reconciliation Act of 1996 (PRWORA), which changed the name of family welfare from AFDC to TANF, limits families to five years on the rolls and allows states to curb eligibility for aid in ways they could not before. They may now deny assistance to unwed mothers under 18 or to children born to mothers already on the rolls. PRWORA also ended the federal entitlement to aid. Henceforth, Washington will not finance aid for all persons eligible for it, but only make a block grant to states that does not change with the number of aid claimants.[2]

But in any thoroughgoing form, terminating aid is impolitic. The public may reprove existing welfare as permissive, but it strongly opposes throwing the needy on the street. States are highly unlikely to deny aid to any important group of recipients that is now covered, even if federal funding is no longer assured for all of them. The politics of welfare leaves government little option except to try to enforce work as part of the welfare system, not instead of it.

I also believe that abandoning dependent persons to the marketplace would do more to increase hardship than raise work levels. Merely to deny aid does not tell people what they should do instead of being dependent. It is not prescriptive enough. The behaviour of seriously poor adults seems to respond more strongly to direction from public authority than it does to economic incentives. It may be that enforcing work within welfare will prove to be beyond the capacities of American government, for reasons I discuss below. Then the abolition of aid might become the best course, the only feasible reform. It is too early to conclude this today.

At the other extreme are traditional liberal proposals to overcome poverty without solving the work problem, simply by transferring income to the poor. In the 1960s and 1970s liberals proposed to do this by liberalising the welfare system to cover parts of the low-income population besides female-headed families. A more recent proposal is to pay families a $1,000 refundable tax credit for each child under 18. This would be less controversial than welfare, the argument runs, because the benefit would be universal, akin to social security, and would not go just to those who are poor.[3] A similar idea is to expand the child support system to provide more income to fatherless families, again for the entire population. If the father did not pay support, an assured benefit would be paid to the mother. It is also claimed that the assured benefit would raise work effort among welfare mothers because it would not be reduced if they worked, as welfare is.[4]

These proposals are no more politic than abolishing welfare. Currently, they are probably unaffordable, given the federal budget deficit. More fundamental, the public has made clear that it will not countenance giving more money to poor families until the parents do more to help themselves. Past liberal welfare reform proposals were defeated in Congress mainly because they did not contain serious work requirements,[5] and this would likely be the fate of the recent proposals if any president espoused them. The idea that the new benefits are universal is unpersuasive unless those who are poor, like social security beneficiaries, earn them through employment, but the plans do little to raise work levels. The child tax credit is not, like the EITC, conditioned on employment.[6]

Child support is supposedly earned by the father. But because poor fathers usually do not work enough to pay their judgements, their families would have to be supported by the assured benefit, which is welfare under another name. The work incentives implicit in the scheme would not cause many mothers to work.[7] On the contrary, the main effect of the scheme might be to free the mothers from the work requirements that are now tightening in TANF. They could shift from welfare to assured child support and escape any serious pressure to work.

Lately, some liberals have tried to combine increased aid with more serious work requirements by proposing to time-limit cash welfare and follow it with government jobs. Adult recipients could draw aid without work for two or three years, after which they would have to take a private job or accept one provided by government.[8] This was the proposal that Bill Clinton offered, following his election as president in 1992 on a promise to 'end welfare as we know it'. The Clinton welfare plan would have limited families to two years of aid without work, after which parents would have had to take jobs. However, they would have been guaranteed a government job if necessary, and there was no overall limit on the duration of aid. This plan was overtaken by more severe Republican proposals, leading to PRWORA's five-year limit and other curbs on welfare eligibility.

A more extreme liberal position is to abolish cash assistance entirely and offer the poor only government jobs, which would presumably drive most applicants to work in the private sector. To hand out jobs instead of cash sounds like the simple, direct solution to the work problem, because it ensures that anyone assisted is working for his or her benefits.[9] In principle, I support this idea, but it is impractical. Government jobs cost much more than simply paying people aid. The idea would be strongly opposed by civil service unions, who fear welfare recipients competing for regular government jobs. Simply to guarantee work to all recipients still on the rolls after two years of aid might require 1.5 million positions and cost $40 billion a year.[10] It was largely to avoid this cost that the Clinton planners decided to impose their two-year limit only on welfare mothers born in 1972 or later. That considerably reduced the appeal of the Clinton plan. And, as mentioned above, recent experience with government-created jobs is not encouraging.

5

The Case for Work Requirements

PROGRAMMES THAT require work of the dependent look a lot more promising than any voluntary solution to the work problem. Largely for this reason, welfare reform in the United States has principally endeavoured to stiffen these requirements.

The Drive for Enforcement

Since the late 1960s, Washington has tried to use the welfare system to enforce work by requiring employable recipients to seek work or enter training as a condition of support. The first work enforcement instrument was the Work Incentive (WIN) programme, enacted in 1967. It mandated that welfare mothers work if judged employable by welfare agencies and, later, if their youngest child was at least six. Due to limited funding and authority, WIN had no discernible effect on welfare work levels or caseloads.

The Family Support Act of 1988 (FSA) aimed to strengthen work requirements by setting up the more ambitious Job Opportunities and Basic Skills Training Program (JOBS). States were required to involve 20 per cent of their employable recipients (now defined to mean mothers with no child under three) in JOBS on a monthly basis by 1995 or face cuts in their federal welfare funding. States in turn could require the clients to enter these programmes on pain of cuts in their grants. Funding was increased for JOBS and also for the childcare and other support services needed to put welfare mothers to work. Whereas WIN served about 145,632 recipients a year at its height in 1980, JOBS by 1994 served 445,632 every month, or more than six times the WIN level on an annual basis.[1]

PRWORA, the new welfare law, sets still more severe requirements. It mandates adult recipients to work within two years of

23

going on aid and demands that states move half of them into 'work activities' by the year 2002. Interim targets are set for the intervening years. The base for calculating participation is now all cases, not an 'employable' subset, who were about half the cases under JOBS, although states may exempt mothers with a child under one year. Thus, compared to JOBS, both the participation norm and the share of clients obligated are about doubled, so the mandate is about four times as tough as before. And whereas in JOBS most participants entered education or training in preference to immediate work, in PRWORA 'work activities' is defined to mean mainly actual work in regular or subsidised jobs. The hours of activity required to count as a participant rise from 20 hours a week, as in JOBS, to 30 hours by 2000.

Effects of Work Programmes

These ambitious standards reflect a positive evaluation history. The Manpower Demonstration Research Corporation has been evaluating mandatory welfare/work programmes for more than a decade. Table 6 (p. 54) shows the average impacts recorded in the nine principal evaluations finished by MDRC to date. Effects are expressed in terms of how much earnings and employment rose, or AFDC payments or dependency fell, for clients in the programme compared to equivalent clients not in the programme. While the effects are generally too small to overcome the welfare problem, the programmes do make a meaningful contribution to raising employment and reducing dependency.

Although most of the programmes did not reduce the welfare rolls by much, they did save money for government, because the reductions in grants as clients went to work more than paid for the costs. The common idea that reforming welfare through work costs more than just paying out aid fails to allow for these savings. The programmes have also been notably untroubled by the various barriers that many analysts suppose prevent the poor from working. Lack of jobs or childcare has not been a major impediment in most localities.[2]

The most successful of these programmes, furthermore, have recorded effects that, by any measure, are more than marginal. Table 7 (p. 55) shows the impact of the three most notable programmes evaluated by MDRC, all in California. The first San Diego programme, which was the first to show definite effects on welfare, had a strong influence on the enactment of JOBS in 1988. SWIM—an experimental programme that attempted to maximize participation—did still better. Riverside was the leading county in MDRC's evaluation of six counties operating California's JOBS programme, known as Greater Avenues for Independence, or GAIN. Riverside raised earnings by two-fifths and employment by more than a quarter, while reducing dependency by enough to yield a clear profit for government.

The effects on lifestyle have been still larger than the economic impacts. Recipients subject to work programmes participated in *some* employment-oriented activity—whether training, working, or looking for work—at about twice the rate of recipients not so subject. The multiple for participation in job-search—which many clients avoid in preference to education or training—was about six times.[3] Thus, welfare/work programmes can make a welfare caseload pay serious attention to self-improvement, even if only some recipients leave welfare in the short run.

The Need for Mandatoriness

Why should we attribute these effects to *requiring* recipients to work? Perhaps good results followed simply from funding programmes that provided needed new services, on a voluntary basis. It is true that Congress has never specifically required that state work programmes be mandatory, in the sense of requiring participation as a condition of aid. The programmes could be voluntary provided the states met the participation standards set out in FSA or PRWORA. Until recently, most experts on these programmes tended to favour voluntariness. The programmes could be effective, it was felt, only if they motivated recipients to participate by what they had to offer, without any mandate.[4]

It was also politic in the early stages of work enforcement to leave it ambiguous whether programmes were mandatory. Conservatives demanded that states be forced to do something about work, while liberals demanded that the programmes be conceived mainly as aid to the recipients, not coercion. Under WIN and JOBS, participants were placed in education or training as much or more than in job-search. People referred to the programmes were made to participate in *some* activity, not usually to go to work immediately. Once involved in the programme, participants themselves chose to take a job more often than they were 'forced' to by government.

But under PRWORA that is bound to change. The new law is much more explicit about requiring work. Welfare parents now have to work within two years of going on aid, and states face such demanding work standards that they could not meet them without enforcing work on their recipients. This shift reflects not only the conservative politics of the recent reform, but what scholars have learned about raising work levels. It has become clear that effective work programmes must be highly prescriptive and authoritative.

One clear finding is that high participation in programmes is essential to show results. On a voluntary basis, work programmes would have low participation, since few welfare recipients volunteer for them. Many clients drop out or fail to appear at programmes even when assigned to them. However, the most noted programmes, such as those summarised in Table 7 (p. 55), all achieved high participation. Statistical analyses show that the higher the participation rate in a local or state programme, the higher the proportion of clients that enters jobs, even controlling for differences in the employability of the clients and the labour market.[5]

The three programmes summarised in Table 7 were all notably tough about insisting that people assigned to them show up and participate regularly. They followed up on clients who failed to appear, and they speedily 'sanctioned' those—that is, reduced their welfare grant— who failed to cooperate. Once expectations are clear, the vast majority of clients comply with them. Through intense monitoring and follow-up of clients, SWIM achieved monthly participation rates of around half and yearly rates of three quarters, about the highest ever recorded.[6] No voluntary policy has shown anything like this effect on lifestyle.

Under SWIM or Riverside GAIN, welfare is not ended, but its nature is transformed. The system now seriously requires that dependent persons improve themselves as a condition of support. Going on welfare becomes like going into the army. Those who qualify receive undoubted financial support and other benefits, but in return they have to function in clear-cut ways. It is the obligation to participate in a programme that primarily motivates recipients to organise their private lives for work and then to move into employment, although support services are also necessary.

One reason that participation matters is that it exposes more of the clients to the programme. To the extent participation is reduced, so is impact, assuming the programme is worth anything to the clients. Another reason is that raising participation tends to bring into the programme precisely those clients most likely to benefit from it. If a programme is voluntary, the recipients who participate tend to be the most employable and motivated, those who would go to work even without a programme. These clients generate appealing success stories, but to serve them produces little change from what would otherwise occur. Enforcing participation brings in more reluctant and disadvantaged clients, those likelier to benefit. It is these recipients, from below the 'cream', who produce most of a programme's impact.[7]

The Need for Actual Work

A further conclusion from the research is that effective programmes not only enforce participation, they insist that participants actually work or look for work. In the early years of work enforcement, raising participation was paramount and the nature of that participation seemed secondary. As noted, both WIN and JOBS emphasized education and training more than they did actual work. But when participation finally rose above the minimal, as it did during the implementation of JOBS, it became clear that the better programmes insisted on 'work first'. The three programmes in Table 7 (p. 55) all had this character.

The national evaluation of JOBS, now being conducted by MDRC, provides the first direct test of a work-oriented strategy against an education-and-training strategy in welfare employment. The first approach stresses 'labour force attachment' (LFA), or job-search followed, if necessary, by an unpaid job or short-term training. The other emphasises 'human capital development' (HCD), or education and training in advance of work. In preliminary results after two years, clients in LFA recorded markedly larger gains in employment and earnings, and greater economies in welfare, than did clients in HCD.[8]

One reason might be that the work approach gets clients into jobs quickly while the education-and-training approach puts them in school where they have less chance to earn money in the short run. Perhaps the investment that HCD makes in skills will eventually pay off in its clients getting 'better' jobs. Among several 1980s programmes evaluated by MDRC, one in Baltimore with a training emphasis actually recorded the largest earnings gains five years after the programme began, even more than San Diego's SWIM.[9] And in MDRC's GAIN evaluation, although Riverside was generally superior, other counties oriented more to training and education began to show similar earnings increases by the third year of the programme, perhaps because their investments in skills had begun to bear fruit.[10]

However, SWIM realised large savings in welfare while Baltimore achieved none, and Riverside clearly outperformed the other counties in the GAIN study in reducing welfare. The earnings gains in training-oriented programmes appear not to translate well into welfare reductions, chiefly because the gains are concentrated among the more advantaged recipients who leave welfare quickly even without a programme. These clients generate little welfare savings when compared to similar controls. Work-oriented programmes are more able actually to shorten welfare stays.[11]

Willingness to enforce participation and work is the main policy feature that distinguishes a SWIM or Riverside. These programmes were well-funded compared to some others studied by MDRC, but not as well-funded as some of the training-oriented projects. SWIM spent $643 per client, whereas Baltimore spent $953. In GAIN, Alameda and Los Angeles Counties spent much more per client than Riverside, mainly because they invested more heavily in education and training. Yet SWIM and Riverside generally performed better. The demanding, work-oriented programmes also saved more money for government because of their ability to reduce welfare.[12] However, some portion of this superiority is due not to policy but rather to the well-run character of the San Diego and Riverside programmes, a factor that I return to below.

Diversion

Even the results of a SWIM or Riverside only begin to suggest how work enforcement might change welfare. Evidence has appeared recently that tough work programmes can reduce dependency by much more than the evaluations suggest. The reason is that evaluations capture only the effects programmes have on clients who are already in the programme, which generally means on welfare. They cannot capture the tendency of tough work requirements to keep people off welfare entirely. Robert Moffitt has argued that welfare/work programmes might either raise or lower entry to welfare. They might attract people onto welfare if they were good at training people for 'better' jobs—or keep them off if they were severe. On plausible assumptions, full implementation of a mandatory programme like JOBS might reduce the caseload by as much as 25 per cent.[13]

Wisconsin may well have brought that possibility to pass. This state has been reforming welfare for more than a decade.[14] It began implementing JOBS-like work requirements in AFDC in the mid-1980s, even prior to the enactment of JOBS. It also implemented JOBS well, achieving participation rates far above those mandated by the law. Then, in the early 1990s, it reoriented JOBS away from education and training and towards putting clients to work in available jobs. Between 1987 and 1997 it reduced its AFDC caseload by more than half, much the largest decline of any state. Statistical analyses suggest that the fall was due to both the state's favourable economy, which generated many jobs, and its demanding work programmes, which drove many employable recipients off the rolls.[15]

In 1994-96 the state instituted experimental work programmes in selected counties that attempted to divert families from welfare. When people entered welfare offices to apply for aid, they were intercepted by staff who tried to persuade them to get a job immediately or seek help from relatives rather than go on welfare, even if they were eligible for it. They could still apply for aid, but then they were required to look for jobs while their applications were processed. And if aid were approved and accepted, they would be referred immediately to a work-oriented JOBS programme, where again they would have to look for work.

According to state and local officials, counties with these policies sharply reduced their intake to the rolls. The effect was to accelerate the ongoing decline in dependency. The caseload, which had already fallen 25 per cent between January 1987 and the end of 1994, fell another 26 points by October 1996, for a 51 per cent decline overall. Even Milwaukee's caseload, the largest and most troubled in the state, has come down by a quarter.[16] While some of the credit goes to a tight labour market, such figures again imply that the effects of work requirements on dependency are potentially much larger than the evaluations suggest.

6

The Future of Work Enforcement

THE SUCCESS of work programmes in recent years explains why work enforcement has become the leading theme in American welfare policy, at both the federal and state levels. At the time it was superceded by PRWORA, JOBS had become the best-funded federal training programme and the main force driving localities to innovate in welfare. Its implementation had been slowed in many states by inadequate local funding, among other problems.[1] Nevertheless, the JOBS participation mandates have already forced big-city welfare programmes to start building employment into their routines as never before. Participation clearly is a lever that, if pressed, can force real change in the welfare régime.

It was clear by 1995 that the JOBS participation targets would have to be raised well above 20 per cent on a monthly basis to maintain this momentum. JOBS also gave too much priority to education and training over actual work. PRWORA goes far toward redressing both problems—maybe too far. As mentioned, the participation norm is raised by about four times, and the activity demanded is now largely actual work. And although many states found JOBS' 20 hour-per-week participation standard difficult, PRWORA raises it to 30.

On their face, these targets look impossible, as they are much tougher than any work programme has achieved.[2] In the next year or two the participation thresholds may be achievable because states may count against them any percentage by which their caseloads dropped after 1995, and caseloads are currently falling. But after that, many states will have difficulty meeting the targets unless caseloads continue to fall. The same with the 30-hour participation standard. Much will hinge on how details of the requirements are defined in regulations.

One issue is resources. Under PRWORA, there is no specific funding for work programmes, since the old JOBS money is folded into the block grant. On the other hand, states receive a windfall in the short run, since allocations under the block grant presume the caseloads of 1995, which were higher than currently. States cannot ignore the work rules for, if they fail to satisfy them, they face cuts in their TANF grants of as much as 21 per cent.

Another issue is job availability. As mentioned earlier, the labour market has to date been a minor constraint on most work programmes. Limitations on the programmes' internal capacity and authority were more important than lack of jobs or childcare. Under TANF, the level of activity may finally rise to where it begins to put pressure on those markets, especially jobs. Must government contemplate the need to create jobs for the dependent? To date, most work programmes have been able to place the great majority of clients in the private sector and have needed only a small pool of public positions as a backup for the hard-to-employ. Clinton, who provided government jobs in his welfare proposal, now advocates new tax incentives to promote the hiring of recipients in private business. Short of a severe recession, that is a better strategy than public job creation.

How Enforcement Works

The next question is how mandatory programmes produce their effects. What is it about levying a requirement to work that motivates recipients to get a job or leave welfare? Experimental evaluations can tell us little about this. These studies tell if a whole programme has an effect, but not what activities within the programme produced it. To find out how a programme works, one has to get inside the 'black box' by using a combination of field research and programme data analysis.[3]

Enforcing Participation and Work

Why do *requirements* cause recipients to participate and work where merely offering them the chance to does not? Recipients appear to need a 'push' from the public authority to realise their own desires to work.

Most staff members of welfare employment programmes I have interviewed say participation in a work programme must be mandated to get recipients' attention. Most adults on welfare would like to work in principle, but they are pre-occupied with day-to-day survival. Few will make the initial effort to organise themselves for regular activity outside the home unless it is required.[4] Entry into work or job-search must also be enforced, many staff say, because recipients are often reluctant to seek work on their own. They usually have failed to find or keep jobs before—especially 'good' ones able to take them off welfare—and they are fearful to try again. Many prefer education and training because it is less threatening. It postpones the day when they must reckon with the labour market.

Even with a mandate, programmes find achieving participation and work is difficult. When summoned to enroll in a programme, many recipients fail to appear. Even if they do, they often disappear later when referred on to a specific activity, or 'component'. Every time clients are referred thereafter, some drop out. The disadvantaged often respond to external challenges with withdrawal. To obtain and maintain involvement, programmes must get out the word that participation is not a formality. When first implemented, they often must sanction many recipients for non-participation, until the word spreads 'on the street' that the programme is serious.

Opponents of work enforcement think that tough programmes go on sanctioning heavily, that much of their impact results from throwing people off the rolls. It is true that effective programmes such as SWIM or Riverside are very willing to sanction, and they advertise this to their clients. But, in fact, little of the welfare savings that programmes generate is due to sanctions; getting people off welfare by other means is far more important.[5] And at the local level, sanctioning is actually inverse to performance: programme offices that sanction many clients place fewer people in jobs than those that sanction fewer. The reason appears to be that programmes that have to 'throw the book' at non-co-operators have failed to exert authority in more effective and informal ways. Typically, they have failed to make expectations clear to clients up front.[6]

Among several counties I studied in Wisconsin in 1994-95, Kenosha and Sheboygan were the toughest about enforcing participation and work. I contrasted them to four other counties, including Dane (the city of Madison) and Milwaukee, that were more loosely run and emphasised education and training over

immediate employment. In a given month, Kenosha and Sheboygan had the highest rates of enrollment, that is the highest
percentage of recipients referred to them who come in the door.
They also had lower proportions than average in unproductive
holding statuses between activities. Because they were tough
about enforcing job-search, they had the highest proportions
actually working—about 40 per cent in regular or unpaid jobs.
Yet they had only one per cent of their clients sanctioned for non-
co-operation, well below the norm. The effect of making expectations clear was not to repel the clients but to involve and
motivate them.[7]

Enforcement and Performance

Involvement, in turn, promoted performance. During 1993,
Kenosha and Sheboygan placed more than a quarter of all their
clients (both enrolled and non-enrolled) in jobs, and over a third
of recipients still on the rolls were employed, levels far above the
four other counties. Yet these counties were competitive with the
other counties in the quality of jobs their participants obtained,
as measured by wages and retention rate, meaning the share of
job entrants who kept their jobs for 30 or 180 days. This was
true even though the other counties concentrated on getting
'good' jobs by training participants prior to placement. Kenosha
appeared able to combine quantity with quality of jobs by
stressing a combination of work and training. Recipients were
told to get a job—any job—*and then* they could train for a better
job as well. This 'work first' sequence reversed the order in most
other counties in Wisconsin and in the JOBS programme
nationally, where education or training tended to substitute for
work.[8]

One might suspect that Kenosha and Sheboygan performed
well because their clients were unusually employable or their
labour markets favourable. But the association of enforcement
with performance held up even controlling for the environment.
I constructed statistical models to predict variations in the JOBS
performance measures across all 72 Wisconsin counties in 1993.
The proportions of a county's clients that entered jobs, worked
while on welfare, or closed their cases was determined largely by
the shares that enrolled (that is, participated), entered job-
search, or went through job-readiness, a component that teaches

the skills and motivation for job-search. Demographic and economic conditions were secondary. Enforcing participation and work did not much improve the quality of jobs which clients obtained; that was much more a function of their education and other human capital. The programme, however, substantially controlled whether its clients went to work in *some* job.[9] Counties that implemented JOBS well also recorded a faster caseload decline between 1986 and 1994.[10]

Case-management

Effective work programmes do more than impose a formal requirement to participate and work. They implement it through staff members who monitor clients closely to be sure they fulfill their obligations. States running JOBS invested in case managers in order to raise client involvement in JOBS and meet the participation mandates in FSA.[11] Analysts tend to view case managers as a service to clients. One important role they have is helping to arrange the services, such as childcare, that mothers need to participate.

Effective programmes, however, also use case managers in a directive way. They are the chief means of countering the tendency of clients to drop out. They check up on participants to make sure they are still in the programme. When people disappear, they pursue them to get them to come back. They call them up, send them letters, go out and visit their homes, if necessary begin proceedings to sanction. In leading programmes, this follow-up is relentless. 'Making them active, tracking them, not letting them sit there in limbo'—this was what got people moving, one case manager in Sheboygan told me. Riverside's JOBS director remarked, 'It's really simple: you've got to be all over every client like flypaper! Every day'.[12] In top programmes, case managers claim to know what the majority of their clients are doing every day. At its best, case-management combines help and hassle.

Personalised attention is what makes expectations clear and allows the demanding programmes to reduce sanctions once they have raised participation to acceptable levels. Kenosha, for example, had few clients sanctioned, but it had many clients in 'reconciliation', a process by which non-co-operators were talked into returning to the programme and thus avoiding sanctions.

Intense interaction between clients and staff is a feature of effective work programmes.[13]

At the same time, case-management is not social work in the sense of intimate involvement in the lives of clients. That would be too demanding for staff to sustain for long periods. It would lead to 'burn-out', a problem for many professionals who deal with the poor.[14] Mainly, case-management is rule-enforcement. Staff do have to relate to their clients as individuals, not as numbers, but mainly they check up on them. Just doing this appears to be strongly motivating.

Monitoring

The case managers need help to do their tracking. Some welfare employment programmes invest in elaborate management information systems to follow the movements of their clients. Computers can record the activities to which the participants have been assigned, such as job-search, unpaid work, or education or training. They cannot determine whether the clients are actually engaging in these activities. To know that requires feedback from the staff running those functions, often employed by outside contractors. This information is often relayed back to the case managers on paper or over the phone, outside the computer. Effective programmes have well-greased arrangements for taking and reporting attendance. Some even use their own staff for the function, or pay others to perform it.

The monitoring systems are also essential for higher-level management. Supervisors need to know where clients are referred and how many get jobs or leave welfare in order to hold their case managers accountable. Analysis of the figures can suggest which activities are most productive. Senior executives have to be able to compare the performance of offices, and to report evidence of results to elected officials. Few welfare/work programmes today have information systems able to perform all these tasks.

How Clients Respond

To welfare advocates, mandatory work requirements appear severe. They charge that programmes 'force' or 'coerce' recipients to work. Conservative critics of welfare, on the other hand, see

little point in trying to enforce work in the teeth of the disincentives to work that they think deter employment on welfare. Better
to abolish aid so that the employable have no alternative to
working. Both viewpoints assume that the recipients have in
some sense *chosen* not to work.

When asked, however, most welfare recipients and other poor
people typically say that they want to work. If they do not
actually work, the reason is that the practical difficulties seem
overwhelming, not that they reject the idea. Not working, in fact,
causes them shame and discouragement, since they are not
living by their own values.[15] This gap between the intention and
behaviour is what makes work enforcement necessary. But the
acceptance of the work ethic also makes it possible. Mandatory
work programmes do not ask most people to do something alien
to them.

The programmes operate precisely to close the gap between
norm and lifestyle. Without enforcement, the recipients are free
to avoid work because of the difficulties. Mandatory programmes
take that option away. They place people in a situation where
they get needed help to work, but they also have to work. They
now have to do what they always wanted to do. The combination
of help and hassle promotes employment as neither voluntary
benefits nor a denial of aid can do.

Most participants respond with gratitude, not resistance. In
several of the programmes MDRC studied, evaluators did surveys
of recipients who were made to 'work off' their benefits in unpaid
government jobs. This sort of assignment, commonly called
'workfare,' is the most punitive of the several activities possible
within most work programmes. The vast majority of respondents
understood work as mandatory, not voluntary. Yet in most cases,
a majority said they were satisfied to work for their welfare rather
than not work, and most felt better about receiving welfare as a
result. Majorities also liked their jobs, felt they were treated like
regular employees, and felt the experience would help them get
a 'decent-paying' job later. The one dissatisfaction was that most
clients felt they gained less from their assignments economically
than did the agencies they worked for; they would have preferred
regular jobs.[16]

These responses indicate that the psychology of welfare is not
middle-class. Better-off people generally behave according to

their own intentions. If they do not do something, it is because they do not want to. They will resist anyone telling them to do otherwise. Middle-class analysts too readily assume that poor people also are consistent. If they do not work, we naturally think they also 'choose' not to, given their situation. But for most welfare adults, non-work is felt as a dilemma, not a choice. They want to work, yet most do not work. When a work programme enforces work, the vast majority accept the requirement. They see it as a help. Work enforcement *assumes* that behaviour is inconsistent, not goal-oriented. It works to make behaviour more consistent.

Many welfare poor seem to be looking for that structure. The idea of case managers monitoring one's behaviour strikes many better-off people as severe. They compare that relationship with authority to the warmer, more affirming relationships they have known. For the poor, however, supervision is often an improvement. In their formative experiences, authority figures commonly treated them harshly and inconsistently. At least case managers generally seek the good of the client, a good he or she can recognize. Above all they are consistent. They enforce a set of rules. They can be satisfied if one obeys the rules. The situation gives the clients more sense of control than they have just living on welfare.

Thus, most recipients respond positively to oversight. It helps them live by their own values. It honours them with the assumption that their behaviour matters. They take it as a form of caring. As one recipient described the people running her training programme: 'They don't want anyone to fail... They're always keeping an eye on you. They're behind you pushing.'[17] To get personal attention of any positive kind is more than many recipients have known. So contact with staff is affirming, and the more the better. 'Contact! ... Once a week, twice a week, there's no such thing as too often,' said one supervisor in Riverside; 'it reminds them that you *care*, and that you're *watching*.'[18]

Diversion and Direction

This positive response to authority helps explain why diversion can be an effective way to drive down the welfare rolls. To suspicious observers, the idea of talking poor people out of welfare sounds like nothing more than denying access to aid. It seems to be a way of restoring to case workers the personal discretion to give or deny aid that they lost as a result of the welfare-rights movement of the 1960s.

But as practised in Wisconsin, diversion does not deny access. At least, it is not supposed to.[19] Rather, diversion staff are directive. They tell applicants what they *ought* to get a job or help from families instead of going on welfare. They also tell them the obligations they will face *if* they go on aid. In response, many in fact avoid welfare. The directive stance clearly is motivating. Whether those who avoid welfare are really better off as a result is much less clear, as I note below.

The whole political climate surrounding welfare reform in Wisconsin is a form of direction. In the course of advocating their reforms, the governor and other officials declare publicly that in future the adults on welfare will be expected to function. This does not mean that all aid is denied. The state is about to institute a new, work-based aid system that will give quite a lot of assistance to the needy. But the message is, you will have to work to get that aid. Public officials, in the name of the society, are telling the poor how to live.

The poor respond, at least to the extent that many leave welfare. According to welfare officials in the state, the moment controversies began about Governor Tommy Thompson's 'learn-fare' proposal in 1987, recipients began leaving the rolls. That programme was not even directed to reducing welfare, at least in the short run. Rather, it required that welfare parents keep their children in school as a condition of aid. But the message of responsibility could not be confined to it. Recipients even outside learnfare heard a call to be more self-reliant, and some left welfare as a result.

The diversion effects that surround welfare reforms pose problems for evaluating them, because it becomes difficult to delimit a programme's influence in space or time. Recipients subject to one programme may respond to another. A reform may begin to influence the rolls as soon as it is publicly discussed, long before it is implemented or even enacted. In Wisconsin, welfare reform has become an ongoing process where the initiatives can no longer be separated from one another, or from an overarching political direction. The governor proposes and the legislature enacts change after change. Some proposals may be half-baked, but they are made anyway to keep the ball rolling. Each reinforces, and is reinforced by, a rhetoric of self-reliance. To assess such programmes discretely or in narrow economic terms is to miss much of the dynamic that drives them.

7

An Assessment of Work Enforcement

WHAT ARE the pros and cons of work requirements in welfare? We must assess the ideas of work enforcement and close supervision, but also to some extent welfare/work programmes in general. There are pluses and minuses, but more important than any concrete drawbacks are the assumptions that this strategy makes about institutional capacity.

Advantages

The economic case for paternalism follows from the impacts work programmes achieve. While voluntary, service-oriented programmes realise some gains, these policies are sometimes not cost-beneficial. They cost too much for the work gains and welfare reductions they realise. It is the mandatory, work-oriented form of welfare employment programme that clearly delivers the goods. The impacts of such programmes are likely to rise as they are more fully implemented. They are a worthwhile investment from any viewpoint.

While many investments might be made in the poor, a virtue of welfare enforcement is that it directly addresses non-work, the greatest economic problem of welfare adults. And it does so in a way that does not immediately deny them all support. The combination of aid with work-tests does more for the dependent than either aid without expectations, the traditional liberal recommendation, or the denial of aid favoured by anti-government conservatives. This combination is also most politic. The voters want welfare adults to do more to help themselves, but not at the cost of putting children at risk.[1] The only way to realise both goals is to enforce work *within* the welfare system.

Work enforcement is also more practicable than more ambitious social programmes. Some advocates would have social service providers intervene deeply in families to promote child development and deal with health and abuse problems. Some such programmes have shown encouraging effects on an experimental basis.[2] But it is doubtful that they could be instituted on a wide scale because of the enormous demands they make for talented and committed staff, as well as cost. Mandatory work programmes have some of the same effect because of their directiveness, but are considerably cheaper. Because they stress work enforcement outside the family, they are more staffable and sustainable without 'burn-out'.

Disadvantages

One may say against work programmes that they have not yet transformed the welfare system. Liberals complain that not enough recipients have been helped to work, conservatives that not enough have been required to work. It is still rarer for a welfare adult to be involved in an employment programme than not, to be working rather than non-working. That has started to change in the states leading welfare reform, and it will have to change in other states if PRWORA is implemented seriously. But the nation has a long way to go to realise a working welfare system.

Welfare/work programmes also address only part of the poverty employment problem. Largely, they address the problems of women, but non-work among men is, perhaps, even more important. Many women go on welfare in the first place because the fathers of their children do not support them. Welfare mothers can be required to work in return for receiving welfare benefits. Although some fathers are on TANF and subject to its requirements, the vast majority are not. This makes them difficult to obligate. Welfare makes an effort to reach absent fathers by establishing paternity and collecting child support, but the potential is limited, simply because the fathers often have few earnings to contribute.

A better answer would be to develop a work enforcement structure for disadvantaged fathers parallel to the one that has evolved for welfare mothers. Such a system might emerge from the child support enforcement system. Some localities are experimenting with child support programmes in which fathers in arrears with their payments can be required to participate and go to work, or else pay their judgements, on pain of going to prison. A programme along these lines in Wisconsin has shown encouraging results.[3]

In addition, welfare/work programmes do not address the problem of unwed pregnancy that precipitates many welfare cases. Some conservatives argue that solving that problem is more important than putting the mothers to work. In fact, there is some evidence that work enforcement, among other mandates attached to welfare, reduces the incidence of unwed pregnancy.[4] But work-tests have never been sold on this basis. Government lacks a policy against unwed childbearing mainly because nobody has found one that clearly works. We know something about how to enforce work, but almost nothing about how to confine pregnancy to marriage.

Institutional Conditions

Perhaps most fatefully, welfare paternalism is a highly institutional policy. Some other approaches to poverty, such as maintaining full employment, arouse less controversy. Others, such as work incentives or simple transfers of income to the poor, require little administration. Work enforcement, however, is inherently controversial, and it makes great demands on the bureaucracy.

In a political culture dedicated to freedom, the idea of making people work is inevitably suspect. To levy such demands on recipients who are disadvantaged and, in the majority of cases, non-white is even more explosive. Unease at this has helped to make all work-tests half-hearted, at least prior to PRWORA. Liberals would far rather help people work than require them to. Even conservatives, who do want to enforce work, traditionally preferred to do that by reducing aid rather than through direct governmental requirements. Both sides love to make freedom their instrument, not obligation. If enforcement has gathered pace, it is only because leaders have realised that raising work levels is essential to integrating the poor, and that neither voluntary benefits nor simple cuts in welfare can accomplish that.[5] But this realisation has taken thirty years to dawn.

In order to enforce work, these tensions must be resolved at the federal and lower level. In Washington, they were somewhat resolved in the Family Support Act of 1988, less so in PRWORA, which conservatives rammed through Congress and the White House largely in defiance of liberals. In states, governors and legislatures must agree closely enough to set the details of work policy. The issues are sometimes delegated to the city or county level, where they are no less contentious.

In several urban states with big caseloads, agreement has failed. Democrats will not seriously enforce work, while Republicans refuse to pay for the services and bureaucracy needed for effective programmes. Even though work programmes with bite save money within a few years, governments must invest 'up front', and that can be tough to justify when budgets are tight. The *impasse* over enforcement and costs is a big reason why welfare has so far changed little in New York, Illinois, or most of California.

Welfare employment is also a highly administered policy. Because it is paternalistic, it cannot simply create opportunities and incentives and wait for the recipients to respond. It must explicitly direct them to participate in programmes and to work. That means calling large numbers in to work offices and then supervising their subsequent movements and activities. To say that this takes case managers and reporting systems only hints at the complexities. Those burdens must be shouldered by a bureaucracy that, in many localities, has endured public scorn and drawn few talented employees for decades. Welfare also is an organisation that until recently was attuned mainly to paying out grants accurately. To replace or supplement that mission with the goal of getting people off welfare through work requires a huge shift in bureaucratic culture.[6]

The public pressure to change welfare is too strong to ignore, yet few states are equal to these political and administrative tasks. Something must be done, yet the disagreements and operational problems are too severe for much actually to change. The outcome in many states is ephemeral reforms, where governors announce initiatives and then nothing changes. Either the proposals die in the legislature or in Washington (assuming waivers of normal federal rules are needed). Or if approved, they fritter out amid bureaucratic compromises and incapacity. Welfare is left operating much as before. Some states such as New Jersey have seen several such 'reforms'. Yet welfare in most places remains a flaccid bureaucracy that pays out money to most recipients while expecting very little of them in return.[7]

The moral is that the only true welfare reform means bureaucratic change that reliably moves more clients toward work. Re-labelling welfare as a work programme does not achieve that if nothing changes in the actual administration of welfare. For then, in practice, one ends up exempting most of the clients. Rather, administrative routines must be changed so more recipients have to participate actively in work programmes. And then more of the participants must be required to work rather than do other things short of work. Only this really 'ends welfare as we know it'.

Exemplary Cases

Where welfare actually changes, the locality typically has unusual political and bureaucratic resources. One reason why pathbreaking welfare programmes appeared early in San Diego is that the city was too conservative for work policies to arouse much local opposition. It also had many skilled administrators with experience of running previous employment programmes.[8] In Riverside, the key to change was a talented welfare director with strong local support who built an outstanding organisation. Riverside GAIN is suffused with the work mission and everyone involved—staff and contractors as well as clients—is accountable for performance.

Wisconsin, another exemplar, began with unusual political consensus. The state has an ambitious government with a tradition of generosity and innovation in social policy, yet its political culture is oriented more to obligations than rights. This ethos leads Democrats to support enforcing work in welfare, as they seldom do in other urban states, while Republicans accept a governmental approach to reform rather than just trying to cut welfare. Although Tommy Thompson, the current Republican governor, is the acknowledged leader of reform, change predates his administration and has drawn substantial support from both parties.[9] Leadership is also strong at the local level, where a number of counties and private groups have undertaken reform programmes on their own.

Impatience for quick results has weakened national anti-poverty policy. American 'wars on poverty' tend to be abandoned before they have a chance to succeed.[10] But in Wisconsin, a consensus to reform welfare formed in the mid 1980s and has lasted ever since. Far from fading, the will to change has grown. After a decade of changes, the state is planning, with little dissent, to replace welfare with a work-based aid system in

September 1997. Under 'Wisconsin Works', or W-2, all recipients must work at one of several levels to get assistance. Many subsidised and community jobs will be created to permit this, but health and childcare subsidies will also be extended to the working poor.

Above all, Wisconsin has a superlative bureaucracy, a legacy of the Progressive era and the state's 'good government' tradition. Public service draws talented individuals who willingly shoulder the special problems of running complex work programmes. Where in other states welfare often shuns innovation, in Wisconsin counties compete to run various experimental reform programmes launched by the Thompson administration. Many also have contracted out much of their operations to private and non-profit organisations. Although I estimate that the state has saved $68 million on welfare reform, this is entirely due to the sharp decline in the caseload since 1986. The state has spent millions on work programmes, and much of that investment has gone into the bureaucracy itself.[11]

The result of these resources is that reform actually happens. Wisconsin is not unusual in what the governor or other politicians say about welfare. Rather, it is unusual in its capacity to execute, to deliver change 'on the ground'. The implementation of JOBS and its later evolution changed palpably how recipients were treated at the local level. As the programme shifted from remediation to a work-first strategy, between 1993 and 1995, its administration tightened and the assignment of clients shifted sharply toward job-search and actual work. As the state prepares for W-2, the share of clients subject to new requirements to 'earn' their benefits with specified activities grows month by month. New routines have been implemented at a rate that counts as speed-of-light for bureaucratic change. Driven by administrative muscle and the economy, the caseload continues to fall. Welfare reform, in short, follows from successful institutional change.

8

The Political Dimension of Workfare

ONE MIGHT attribute the vogue for work enforcement simply to a more conservative political climate. In the 1960s and 1970s, two presidents proposed to liberalise the welfare system. Richard Nixon's Family Assistance Plan (FAP) and Jimmy Carter's Program for Better Jobs and Income (PBJI) would have raised welfare benefits and extended welfare coverage from the mostly female-headed families eligible for AFDC to wider populations of needy. After 1980, with more conservative presidents in office and the budget heavily in deficit, such proposals became unimaginable.

Before 1980 the politics of welfare was rights-oriented. Most federal politicians viewed the welfare poor as disadvantaged and anti-poverty policy as a means of easing their burdens. In the Reagan era, in contrast, the 'deservingness' of recipients came under more question and welfare came to seem permissive. Now many politicians asserted that the poor might need aid, but they should do more to 'earn' it, above all by working. The Family Support Act rested on an idea of 'social contract', of requiring recipients to better themselves as a condition of aid.[1] While PRWORA still expresses that sentiment, it also embodies a more traditional, anti-government conservatism in its cuts and block-granting of aid, the urge to 'get welfare out of Washington'.

The main reason work is still not widely enforced is not resistance among the poor, most of whom want *mores* restored in the inner city. Nor is it resistance among the middle class. The popular attitude on poverty is receptive to enforcement. The voters typically want to help the needy, but they also oppose the 'abuses' that are associated with welfare. The trouble with the standard welfare proposals of the right and left is that they violate one or the other side of this public mind. Abolishing or time-limiting welfare threatens the principle of aiding those who are needy, whereas merely increasing transfers does nothing about the abuses. Work requirements within welfare, although difficult to implement, have the hope of doing both—of helping the vulnerable while moving the employable toward work.

At a mass level, the political problem posed by welfare was never dependency as such but the abuses, of which the most important is non-work. As is often remarked, a great many unemployed and retired people live off the government without controversy, and myriad economic interests receive subsidies from Washington. But this 'middle-class welfare' differs crucially from AFDC because the beneficiaries have done something to earn their benefits. They are working or have worked. They can claim an economic function. Equally, if welfare recipients were earning their benefits through some effort on their own behalf, welfare would become more respectable, more like the social insurance programmes. Other aid to needy persons and their families would also become more popular.

In the public mind, to have the recipients contribute to society in some way is much more important than where their support comes from. For most people in America, helping oneself and getting help from government are not opposed but go together. Those who work steadily also get the most aid from government, and those who do not work get little. The middle class justifies its social insurance benefits on the argument that they are earned. The poor get only the scraps from the government's table, primarily because they are unearned. If poor adults worked at higher levels, they would qualify for more support from both the private and public sectors than they do now.[2]

Resistance of the Élites

The political resistance to enforcement, rather, comes from élites. They interpret the poverty problem much more ideologically than the public. Especially at the national level, the political debate has traditionally been about federal spending and economic interventions, not enforcement of *mores* such as work. The usual battle between Democrats and Republicans is over the scale of government, with one side wishing to do 'more' for people through public programmes, the other 'less'. That battle intensified when Ronald Reagan was elected President in 1980 and again when Newt Gingrich and the Republicans took control of Congress in 1994. But authoritative social policies primarily involve changing the nature of government. A more authoritative welfare state may not change the benefits given to dependent persons much at all. Rather, it demands that they do more to help themselves *in return* for aid.

That is not an option that our leadership readily accepts. In Washington, helping those who are poor is still seen as an alternative to their helping themselves, not as a complement. Social policy analysts, most of whom are liberal economists, assume that people who fail in the private sector deserve the most help from government. Conversely, if one demands that those who are poor work, one is taken to mean that government should do nothing for them. PRWORA is commonly interpreted to mean an end to the federal commitment to the poor, when in fact it preserves substantial federal funding and involvement.

Another difficulty is the rights-oriented nature of the political culture, especially among élites. Both left and right naturally seek to address social problems through some version of extending freedom. Liberals want government to give people new opportunities. Conservatives want less government so that the economy can grow faster. Traditionally, neither focused on the behavioural problems that lead to poverty. They both made the competence assumption. The idea that government—certainly the federal government—might have to restore order to society was utterly alien. Authoritative measures may get results, but they sound like tyranny. It is more appealing to keep looking for barriers to getting ahead that more or less government can remove, even if such policies achieve little.[3]

In the last decade, first one party and then the other has favoured a policy of enforcement, but never both together. During the 1980s, most Republicans wanted to use federal rules to require work in welfare, strengthen local law enforcement, and raise standards in the schools. Most Democrats resisted, fearful of burdening the poor with added stigma and failure. During debates on the Family Support Act, it was Republicans who pressed for tougher work requirements, to which Democrats agreed only reluctantly.[4] After 1992, however, many conservatives embraced anti-government versions of reform that mainly reduced aid to unwed mothers and shifted responsibility for welfare out of Washington. The Clinton Administration, which proposed both to require and guarantee work, then seemed firmer about enforcement. Some Democrats resisted the Clinton plans—then were confronted with far more severe proposals once the Republicans conquered Congress.[5] In the event, PRWORA both cuts aid and adds stringent work requirements—which Democratic liberals and advocates now reject as too harsh.

Public Support

On these enforcement issues, the public is hard-line. It wants order restored in cities, even if it is divided on such moral issues as divorce or abortion. In electoral politics, this social order agenda strongly favours conservatives, just as economic issues of economic opportunity and equality favour liberals. Republican charges that Democrats were 'soft' on crime or welfare were a major reason why the GOP controlled the White House for most of the time between 1968 and 1992. Carter in 1976 and Clinton in 1992 were able to break the Republican grip partly because economic concerns dominated those elections but also because they took more conservative stances on crime and welfare than their own parties.[6] With PRWORA, that sentiment has at last dictated work requirements that, if implemented, will transform welfare.

Should the State Enforce Values?

Social policy disputes are often not what they seem. It is sometimes said that the issue is 'values', with conservatives trumpeting the work ethic or law-abidingness and liberals resisting. But liberals also regret non-work and crime. The real division is over the enforcement of values through public authority. Conservatives would have government tell the poor how to live, whereas liberals want to offer them only the chance to get ahead.

On the surface, too, the debate can seem to be about barriers, with conservatives arguing that opportunity is available and liberals denying it. But the underlying issue is not society so much as the moral responsibility of the poor. Conservatives want to hold the downtrodden accountable for their personal behaviour, whereas liberals will not allow this until society is yet further reformed.

Ultimately, the question comes down to the competence one is willing to attribute to poor persons themselves. One side thinks that the needy can cope with life with less aid if only they are expected to; the other side denies it. Both sides project their interpretations onto the environment. Conservatives tend to see opportunity in society because they think people who act rationally in their own interests can overcome any obstacle. Liberals deny opportunity is sufficient, whatever steps are taken to improve it, because to them people who are poor will always be victims. In short, conservatives still believe in the competence assumption, whereas most liberals have tacitly abandoned it. That difference dominates whatever the facts say about barriers.

Enforcement as a Moderate Policy

Enforcement policies may seem to be hard-line, but they actually take a moderate view of these questions. Work enforcers are not as hostile to poor persons, or as optimistic about their self-reliance, as anti-government conservatives who want to abolish welfare. Neither are they as condescending and pessimistic about those who are needy as liberals who want only to build up anti-poverty spending. Work-tests divide the responsibility for overcoming poverty between the government and those who are poor, giving both a role. The former will give benefits and support services provided the latter take steps to help themselves. Enforcement also assumes that benefit recipients have the capacity to satisfy the most basic public expectations, such as working, if not to live fully independent lives. To realise a régime in which the dependent reliably do that is the best that anti-poverty policy can achieve.

Above all else, a solution to the inner city requires a political class willing to commit itself to this moderate position. The views that poor people are totally undeserving or that they are victims of whom nothing can be expected must be exiled to the political fringes. Black politicians, who have the power to veto any anti-poverty strategy, must join with whites in raising expectations for poor members of their group, in the name of integration. Dependency cannot be abolished in the short run, but it can be made less passive. Sufficiency can come to those who are poor the way it has already come to better-off Americans—through a combination of personal effort and government benefits. But for that to happen, poor adults *must* work much more regularly than they do now. There is no alternative.

Table 1
Work Experience of All Heads of Families
1959-1995

	1959	1970	1975	1985	1995
% of all heads who					
Worked at any time:	85	84	80	76	78
Full-year and full-time:	63	63	58	57	57
Did not work:		14	19	23	22
% of female heads who					
Worked at any time:		61	58	63	67
Full-year and full-time	28	32	31	37	42
Did not work:		39	42	37	33
% of married-couple heads who					
Worked at any time:		87	83	79	80
Full-year and full-time:	67	67	63	61	60
Did not work:		11	15	20	20

Table 2
Work Experience of Poor Heads of Families
1959-1995

	1959	1970	1975	1985	1995
% of all heads who					
Worked at any time:	68	55	50	50	52
Full-year and full-time:	31	20	16	16	19
Did not work:	31	44	49	49	48
% of female heads who					
Worked at any time:	43	43	37	40	46
Full-year and full-time	11	8	6	7	13
Did not work:	57	57	63	60	54
% of married-couple heads who					
Worked at any time:	75	62	61	60	59
Full-year and full-time:	38	28	24	25	25
Did not work:	23	37	38	38	41

Note for tables 1 and 2:

Full-year means at least 50 weeks a year, full-time at least 35 hours a week. Married-couple heads means male heads in 1959-75, heads other than single mothers in 1985, and the husbands of married-couple families in 1995. Some figures do not add due to rounding or the omission of workers in the armed forces.

Source for tables 1 and 2:

Data are from US Department of Commerce, Bureau of Census, Series P-60, no. 35, tables 3 and 13, and no. 68, table 8 (for 1959); no. 81, table 20 (1970); no. 106, table 27 (1975); no. 158, table 21 (1985); March 1996 Current Population Survey, table 19 (1995).

Table 3
Employment Status of Persons 16 and over and Family Heads
By Income Level, in Per Cent: 1995

	Persons	All Heads	Female Heads	With Children Under 18 All Heads	With Children Under 18 Female Heads
All income levels					
Worked at any time:	70	78	67	89	73
Full-year and full-time:	44	57	42	66	44
Did not work:	30	22	33	11	27
Income below poverty					
Worked at any time:	41	52	46	58	49
Full-year and full-time:	10	19	13	21	14
Did not work:	59	48	54	42	51

Note: Full-year means at least 50 weeks a year, full-time at least 35 hours a week.

Source: US Department of Commerce, Bureau of the Census, *Current Population Reports*, Series P-60, no. 194 (Washington DC: US Government Printing Office, September 1996), table 3, and March 1996 Current Population Survey, table 19.

Table 4
Employment Status Contrasting Poor and Non-poor 1991

% of Individuals 15 and over who	Poor	Non-poor
Worked at any time:	39.8	72.0
Full-year and full-time	9.0	45.0
% of family heads who		
Worked at any time:	50.4	80.5
Full-year and full-time:	15.8	61.1
% of female family heads who		
Worked at any time:	42.4	76.1
Full-year and full-time:	9.5	54.5
% of families with two or more workers	16.8	62.6

Source: US Department of Commerce, Bureau of the Census, *Poverty in the United States 1991*, Series P-60, no.181 Washington DC: Government Printing Office, August 1992, pp. xiv-xv.

Table 5
Poverty Rates by Employment Status
of Persons 16 and Over and Family Heads, in Per Cent: 1995

	Persons	All Heads	Female Heads	With Children under 18 All Heads	With Children under 18 Female Heads
Overall:	11	11	32	16	42
Worked at any time:	7	7	22	11	28
Full-year and full-time	3	4	10	5	13
Did not work:	22	23	54	61	78

Note: Full-year means at least 50 weeks a year, full-time at least 35 hours a week.

Source: US Department of Commerce, Bureau of the Census, *Current Population Reports*, Series P-60, no. 194, Washington DC: Government Printing Office, September 1996, table 3, and March 1996 Current Population Survey, table 19.

Table 6
Average Results from Nine Main MDRC
Welfare Employment Evaluations

Impact	Control mean	Experimental-control difference	% Change
Average earnings	$1,992	$329	16
Employed at end of final year	28.4%	3.0%	11
Average AFDC payments	$2,409	-$175	-7
On welfare at end of final year	55.2%	-3.1%	-6

Note: Studies are weighted equally. Results are for AFDC, not AFDC-UP, and are for the last full year of the evaluations, which varied from 1 to 3 years in follow-up. 'Percentage change' means the absolute impact as a percent of the control-group mean. Averages for the percentage changes are means of the individual percentage change figures, not calculated from the averages of the control means and experimental-control differences.

Sources: See Table 7

Table 7: Results from Leading MDRC Welfare/Work Evaluations

Study	Outcome in final year	Control mean	Experimental-control difference	Percentage change
San Diego[a] (1982-5)	Average earnings	$1,937	$443	23
	Employed at end of final year	36.9%	5.5%	15
	Average AFDC payments	$2,750	-$226	-8
	On welfare at end of final year	47.9%	-2.0	-4
San Diego SWIM (1985-7)	Average earnings	$2,246	$658	29
	Employed at end of final year	29.3%	5.4%	18
	Average AFDC payments	$3,961	-$553	-14
	On welfare at end of final year	58.7%	-7.4%	-13
Riverside GAIN (1988-93)	Average earnings	$2,552	$1,010	40
	Employed at end of final year	24.6%	6.6%	27
	Average AFDC payments	$3,448	-$584	-17
	On welfare at end of final year	45.8%	-5.2%	-11

[a] Results apply to AFDC applicants in job-search/work experience.

Sources for Tables 6 and 7: Gueron, J.M. and Pauly, E. with Lougy, C.M., *From Welfare to Work*, New York: Russell Sage Foundation, 1991, pp. 142-43; Kemple, J.J., Friedlander, D. and Fellerath, V., *Florida's Project Independence: Benefits, Costs, and Two-Year Impacts of Florida's JOBS Program*, New York: Manpower Demonstration Research Corporation, April 1995, p. ES-16; Riccio, J., Friedlander, D. and Freedman, S., *GAIN: Benefits, Costs, and Three-Year Impacts of a Welfare-to-Work Program*, New York: Manpower Demonstration Research Corporation, September 1994, pp. 120, 122.

Commentaries

Re-inventing Welfare:
A Response to Lawrence Mead

Frank Field

A S USUAL, Lawrence Mead has offered a clear and provocative analysis of some of the key dilemmas faced by welfare reformers across the globe. How far should governments be giving poor people a shove, rather than just a helping hand? Are the root causes of poverty and social exclusion primarily economic—related to the availability of jobs and the incentives to take them—or sociological—stemming from patterns of behaviour which lock individuals, families and communities out of the mainstream? Is compulsion a necessary ingredient of a success-ful welfare-to-work programme?

Professor Mead's starting point is stark: 'We should not conclude that the bulk of poverty or dependency has economic causes' (p. 11). He argues that there are sufficient low-skilled jobs around, that there are no serious economic disincentives to taking them, and that the causes of poverty are behavioural. The defeatism afflicting the poorest US communities, comprised entirely of the dispossessed, is so great that, for many, paid work is a frightening prospect.

It is a compelling analysis, and it is useful to point out the non-economic sources of poverty. One of the downsides of upwards mobility in the post-Attlee years is that streets which would once have contained half a dozen men or women capable of running Rolls-Royce have been stripped of their local talent. This has also eroded the foundation stone of community institu-tions, including the building of financial institutions. Clever people in dead-end jobs used to turn their skills to their neigh-bours' advantage, in so doing building an alternative career. Now, understandably, they move out. They take with them the informal communication links through which many jobs are secured, leaving those remaining even more cut off and reducing their chances of escape still further.

The UK certainly has pockets of severe deprivation, where jobs are scarce and where a culture of 'retreatism' has been established, although nothing like as entrenched as the US. Our new Social Exclusion Unit—which is really a social *inclusion* unit—is designed to examine the inter-locking sources of disadvantage and look at more active measures to help those who are left behind.

But Professor Mead may be overstating his case, at least as far as the UK is concerned. Economic pressures feed directly into poverty in the UK—and perhaps more in the US than he suggests too. Mead's argument is that the jobs are there but that low-skilled men are refusing to take them. Unemployment is now highly regionalised in the UK. It strikes hardest in the inner cities and in what were once the great mining areas, where job opportunities are scarce, while other areas have plentiful opportunities. While the wages of entry-level jobs in this country (i.e. those taken by the previously unemployed) have, according to Paul Gregg and Jonathan Wadsworth at the London School of Economics, been falling in recent years,[1] there is a resistance from some claimants to taking these jobs because they do not pay enough. 'Paying enough' is seen as the level of benefit plus a substantial additional sum. What has, in fact, been happening in Britain over the past few decades among a significant proportion of claimants is a fundamental shift in attitudes towards means-tested support. It is no longer regarded as a port of call for times of distress. For too many it has become a basic income which can be drawn indefinitely.

It is true that the US has been more successful at creating relatively low-level jobs than most other countries—although the UK has not suffered as much by comparison as continental nations. But in both countries, wages at the bottom end of the market have been falling behind the average rate of growth—which hardly fits with an analysis based on people refusing to take jobs.

Also, while half the jobs in the UK are managerial, professional, technical or craft, it would be quite misleading to think most jobs require few if any skills. A recent study showed that lone parents with only a very few qualifications fared better in the labour market than those with none.[2]

One of the central planks of Mead's analysis, that work is the best form of welfare—for individuals, their families and communities—echoes closely the government's view. In the UK, nearly half the low-income population are in households where no-one is in paid work, compared to a fifth in the 1960s. The most powerful weapon against poverty is a job. And while economic growth ensures job creation—the UK's unemployment level is now at a seven-year low—the government can help to direct the benefits of this growth towards those who most need it.

What about the compulsion element? Mead says only a new emphasis on obligation (we might say responsibility) can achieve the desired effects. Only by compelling people out of the 'culture of poverty' can they be helped. He puts it typically clearly: 'the way forward is no longer liberation but obligation' (p. 15).

Mead criticises voluntary approaches for assuming the poor are 'all primed to work', and only need a better chance. Here he is surely right: some of the longest-term unemployed lack the basic work skills and social skills to hold down a job. The numbers of hours spent on job-search has plummeted over time, and drops sharply as the length of time out of work increases. Policy makers need to recognise that the unemployed are not all dashing around all the time in a frantic search for a job.

Mead's view is a useful corrective to the two opposed assumptions about human nature and behaviour which have crippled thinking on British social policy for so long—on the right that the poor deserved to be so because they are lazy, on the left that the poor are immune from the faults of laziness or dishonesty (although why this particular group are thought to be immune from the human failings of everyone else was never quite made clear).

But Professor Mead and I disagree about where the responsibility for the patterns of behaviour which reinforce poverty lies. He points out that the welfare system offers governments a golden opportunity to flag up and underpin the values it wants to promote. I agree. But I also believe that the current operation of the welfare system is a force in the opposite direction, and is in part responsible for the loss of key civic values of work, honesty and thrift. Means-tested benefits have grown in importance as poverty has risen, and, by penalising honesty and savings, act as a drag anchor on society. Mead thinks the system needs a front-on attack on the retreatism and marginalisation of the poor. I think the system must stop encouraging it.

In order to secure public support the welfare system should, of course, demand the same kind of behaviour from its beneficiaries as they rightly expect of the system: openness and a genuine willingness to contribute to society. But I am not as pessimistic as Professor Mead is about the ambitions of the poor. I believe that the majority want to get off welfare but need active help to do so. Imposing sanctions on those who refuse to play ball may be a useful signal of intent—especially if, as he puts it, the 'word gets out' on the streets—but the use of sanctions would represent a failure on our part as much as the individual concerned.

Nevertheless sanctions need to be part of the New Deal. The threat of penalisation begins to affect the culture in which people consider how they should respond and, indeed, what their responsibilities are. They are, then, more of a teaching agent (for they will only ever directly affect a small minority) than a great engine for social change.

Nor are the poor an homogenous group with the same problems and barriers, and so the universal use of penalties and compulsion may be unnecessary. That most important of all political virtues—balance—is required. Our welfare-to-work proposals include an element of compulsion for the under-25s, but stick to a voluntary approach for lone parents. I am convinced that lone parents are a vast untapped resource, and that simply offering a helping hand should result in an immediate response.

Here is an example of how peer group pressure can be changed, and how that change can play an important part in welfare reform. Many single parents already undertake paid work. Offering help back into work to workless single mothers begins to build up a new norm. It becomes normal for most single parents with young children at school to work at least part-time. Then, as children progress to secondary school, more of this cohort—because they are already in work and have shown that they have marketable skills—will be able, if they wish, to go full-time. It might be argued that sanctions might be required for some lone parents. But what is the point of applying sanctions when it is all too often a lack of childcare which prevents large numbers of single parents from working?

Benefits should not be parcelled out without a second thought from government: we need to begin thinking about welfare payments as a contract rather than simple entitlement. Mead argues rightly that signing on for welfare should immediately trigger a sense of active participation in the job-search. As he puts it: 'going on welfare becomes like going into the army' (p. 26). While the particular metaphor may not travel that well, a culture of *joint* endeavour is absolutely central to the Labour government's view of welfare.

But a contractual approach requires greater flexibility than the current system offers. The nature of the 'contract' will inevitably be very different for a 30-year-old single unemployed man and a single mother with four children. Single solutions to the problem of poverty are always doomed, which is why we are looking at ways to deliver a more personalised service.

This brings me to a key point in Mead's analysis: the institutional implications. His descriptions of successful schemes, especially in Wisconsin and California, make it clear that a caseworker-driven approach, combining 'help and hassle', requires talented, well-resourced, committed front-line workers, who are 'suffused with the work mission'. As Mead writes: 'To say that this takes case managers and reporting systems only hints at the complexities' (p. 44). The means of administration hold the key to the revolution he wants.

On a recent UK visit, one of the authors of the Wisconsin reforms, Jean Rogers, made an interesting point about who made the best caseworkers. The state decided to employ intercept staff, who talk initially to people walking into welfare offices about other alternatives—training, help from friends—on the grounds that once people are on the welfare roll, they find it frighteningly difficult to get off. To the legislators' surprise, the most successful interceptors were people who had previously devoted their working day to the mechanics of doling out payments. Ms Rogers believes this is because these workers knew at first hand the corrosive effect of time on the welfare rolls, and were most creative at finding alternative solutions.

The UK government is looking at ways of giving our local benefit offices greater autonomy of action, more scope for innovation, and more incentive to reduce their caseloads by helping people back into work. I believe the vast majority of benefit officers in this country are caseworkers-in-waiting. They simply need the tools. A caseworker-style approach also meshes with the need to combat fraud in the system: front-line staff are best placed to know the scams and the guilty parties, and thereby prevent fraud from entering the system.

The final point I would like to address is the political implication of Mead's analysis. One of the arguments he puts forward for his 'paternalist welfare' is that the taxpayer will only be willing to fund a system which helps the poor on the explicit basis that the poor behave themselves, or rather behave in ways of which they approve. There is something to this, although I believe the taxpayer wants, most of all, a system that works. Spending more and more money while poverty deepens strikes few people as a success story. This is why we are determined to have a policy of zero tolerance towards fraud—a system which rewards the dishonest does not deserve public support—and, above all, a system which works by offering opportunity rather than dependency.

In the long run, I believe taxpayers will only fund a system in which they themselves have an interest, for example through stakeholder pensions and benefits which have been earned. In the US, 'social security', which largely provides pensions, is seen as the 'third rail' of politics: like the third rail of the electric metro system, any politician who tampers with it gets fried.

Mead says this is because the recipients of these social insurance programmes have had a clear economic function, are seen to have 'earned' their benefits, and that unless the recipients of 'welfare'—in the US, spending on benefits for the poor—are seen in the same light, political support will erode still further.

On the other hand, perhaps the reason social security is sacrosanct is because people feel that they have a real stake in it, and a say in how it operates. If the contributors have a bigger role in drawing up the rules, the system will become more stable and more sustainable. Then the system can draw directly on the deep natural resource of civic values. The key goal of welfare reform, then, is inclusion: giving all of us a stake in our nation's future.

Lessons from America:
Workfare and Labour's New Deal

John Philpott

Introduction

'THIS WILL be the Welfare-to-Work Government' proclaimed Tony Blair in his first keynote speech following Labour's landslide victory at the 1997 General Election.[1] Whilst the Prime Minister's terminology is inherited from the United States, Mr Blair would no doubt distance himself from the US term 'workfare' as used by Professor Lawrence Mead with its connotation of unemployed people being forced to work for their Giro cheque. Yet there is a certain resonance between Mead's arguments and the Labour government's employment policy agenda, not least in relation to the so-called New Deal for young unemployed people.

From April 1998 all 18-24-year-olds who have been jobless and on benefit for more than six months will be required to choose between a variety of temporary training-related employment programme options or the option of full-time education or training. But the unconditional right to life on full benefit will be removed and benefit sanctions will be imposed on young people who fail to choose from the available options. The New Deal could therefore be said to conform in some fashion to Mead's broad definition of workfare, i.e. any employment, training or job-search programme which jobless people on benefit are required to attend.

Given the controversy surrounding the benefit sanctions linked to the New Deal, Mead's argument that mandatory jobs programmes are those most successful in reducing long-term welfare dependency—plus what he says about the operation of successful programmes—obviously deserves attention. However, before assessing Mead's case for workfare from the perspective of the current British welfare-to-work debate, one first needs to consider the relevance to Britain of Mead's view that the causes of core joblessness in the US are of a largely non-economic nature.

What Stops Britain's Jobless People From Working?

Mead concludes that only about one third of the jobless poor in the US face identifiable economic or impersonal barriers that prevent them from working. The majority fail to work because of self-defeating attitudes to work which are not sufficiently challenged by public authorities. Mead's argument is not that the jobless poor do not want to work but that inertia or trepidation overcomes their willingness to work. Mead's conclusion is doubtless a source of controversy amongst analysts in the US. But to what extent might it be applicable to jobless people in Britain?

Social differences between Britain and the US mean that caution must exercised when making comparisons. Welfare institutions and benefit coverage differ significantly. Moreover, while some of Britain's ethnic minorities suffer disproportionately from unemployment, the racial dimension of welfare dependency (which is in many ways central to Mead's analysis) is far less marked than in the US. Economic differences are important too. Mead prefaces his study by commenting that a 'depression-like lack of work' is rarely a problem that faces jobless people in the US. This is clearly not true of Britain which has experienced two major recessions since the late 1970s that have resulted in periods of widespread cyclical (i.e. demand deficient) unemployment.

This latter observation appears to limit the overall relevance to Britain of Mead's analysis. Mead's conclusions are thus best assessed in relation to core joblessness of a kind that underlies cyclical fluctuations in economic activity and cannot be reduced by expansionary policies alone (not, at least, without adding to inflationary pressures). In Britain this core problem manifests itself in two main ways: a high level of long-term unemployment and a substantial number of so-called 'workless households'.

In Spring 1997 (the latest period for which data are available at the time of writing) there were 758,000 long-term (i.e. twelve-months-plus) unemployed people in Britain. Although the numbers of long-term unemployed rise and fall during the course of the economic cycle, they nowadays account for a very high proportion of total unemployment. Two decades ago less than 20 per cent of unemployed people were long-term unemployed; today the figure is almost 40 per cent. A rise in structural joblessness is also evident from the non-pensioner workless household rate, which has risen from eight per cent in the mid-1970s to a little under 20 per cent (i.e. one in five households) at present.[2]

Britain's workless household problem offers perhaps the best point of comparison with the socio-economic phenomenon Mead describes in the US. A large proportion of workless households— approximately one in four—are single-parent families, the group on which the US welfare-to-work debate is focused. Moreover, and also drawing some parallel with Mead's analysis, the workless household problem cannot simply be attributed to an overall shortage of jobs in the economy.

For example, the workless household rate has been barely touched by the improvement in the economy and labour market since 1992. Indeed, at around 18 per cent at Winter 1996, the workless household rate was higher than the 17.5 per cent recorded when the recovery began. Similarly, international comparisons of workless household rates show that in Britain the rate is high relative to the overall unemployment rate, indicating a more unequal share of jobs between households whatever the overall state of the labour market.[3]

These facts gives rise to concern that a significant proportion of British households are in effect being excluded from the wider economy and society. However, whilst these households might be said to comprise a British 'underclass', in contrast to Mead's analysis one can attribute the emergence of Britain's workless household problem to a variety of economic and institutional factors that prevent jobless people from taking advantage of available job opportunities. At the root of the problem lies the interaction between structural change in the labour market and the operation of the benefit system which drives up long-term joblessness and limits the ability of people from workless households to move from welfare to work.

Structural Change and Unemployment

Some explanations of persistent joblessness are rooted in ongoing developments in technology and/or trade which have caused the demand for labour to shift away from less skilled or routinely skilled workers towards those who can perform 'problem-solving' jobs. The number of workers classed as labourers, for example, fell by 57 per cent between 1981 and 1991 and, according to current forecasts, will have fallen by a further 38 per cent between 1991 and 2001.[4] In addition many craft and skilled manual jobs have also disappeared as the economy has de-industrialised and shifted toward services. By contrast, as evidence from the 1990s recovery demonstrates, net job creation is strongly biased toward the managerial, professional and technical occupations (these account for roughly three quarters of jobs created since 1993).

Men have borne the brunt of this change. The current male unemployment rate of 8.2 per cent (as measured by the Spring 1997 Labour Force Survey (LFS)) is well above that for women (6.0 per cent). The tendency for the male unemployment rate to exceed the female rate is a long-standing feature of the British labour market (and the opposite of what one observes in most other European Union countries). But the trend over recent years indicates that men have been doing even less well.

The female unemployment rate was lower in Spring 1997 than at its previous low point in Spring 1990 while that for males was up from 6.8 to 8.2 per cent, having been roughly equal to the female rate in 1990. Moreover, the male labour force has contracted during the course of the recovery. In the four years to Spring 1997 the number of economically inactive men increased by 240,000 (a rise of almost 10 per cent; the withdrawal of men from the labour market was equivalent to one third of the fall in male unemployment during that period). Since the late-1970s the proportion of working-age men who participate in the labour market has fallen from over 90 per cent to 84 per cent (for women, by contrast, the participation rate has risen from 63 to 71 per cent).

While it is arguable that the position of men in the jobs market simply reflects an overall shortage of jobs which will resolve itself as the recovery proceeds, there are signs of a deeper structural malaise affecting male employment prospects in Britain. For example, the pattern of job destruction and creation in the 1990s has been strongly biased against men. There is a far greater concentration of men than women in the production industries (including manufacturing) and construction than in the service sectors. The production industries and construction shed relatively more jobs in the recession and (with the exception of construction) have since experienced a jobless recovery.

In the four years to Spring 1997 employment in manufacturing as measured by the LFS fell by over seven per cent. The (working-age) male employment rate fell from 82.7 per cent in Spring 1990 to 75.3 per cent in Spring 1993 and by Spring 1997 had still only recovered to 77.6 per cent. The female employment rate fell from 67.1 per cent to 65.4 per cent in the three years to Spring 1993 but by Spring 1997 had recovered to 67.4 (i.e. just above the previous peak).

Related to the sectoral imbalance in the ebb and flow of jobs is the fact that while men mostly work on a full-time basis on permanent contracts—almost nine out of ten male employees is in a full-time job with a permanent contract compared with only one in two female employees—almost two-thirds of jobs created during the 1990s recovery have been part-time and/or tempo-rary.[5] Whilst there is nothing inherently inferior about part-time or temporary jobs—indeed most people who work in this way in Britain want to do so—it is evident that for one reason or another such jobs do not engage men as easily as women.

The consequences of this shift are not, however, confined to jobless men but extend to their female partners and families as a result of the perversity of the benefit system. Means-tested benefits are assessed on the basis of family incomes. The female partners of unemployed men may therefore find that they will reduce the overall family income if they take a job offering less than sufficient to float the family off benefit completely. Since most jobs being taken by women at present are part-time (and thus do not offer the equivalent of a full-time weekly wage) this effectively shuts the women partners of unemployed men out of the labour market altogether. Hence one reason for the rise in workless households.

Perhaps even more important has been a rise in the number of workless single-parent households. The doubling of Britain's single-parent population to 1.7 million that has occurred over the past twenty years reflects a variety of social developments (albeit here too there may be a link with the changed economic fortunes of men which reduces their attractiveness as marriage-partners and leads more women to raise children on their own). But social factors per se seem unlikely to account for the fact that during the same period the proportion of *workless* single parent families has grown from around one-third to a little under two-thirds. This outcome is far more likely to be explained by economic factors, in particular the difficulty single-parents face in securing work that pays enough to cover necessary childcare costs (assuming, that is, that affordable childcare is available).

The worst manifestation of these workless-household problems are found in depressed localities and inner-city areas where the interaction of structural change and benefit traps is exacerbated by an overall shortage of jobs. Unlike in the US, however, problems of joblessness and urban poverty are not confined almost exclusively to Britain's ethnic minority groups.

Work Incentives and the Benefit System

Mention of pay rates in relation to the operation of the benefit system suggests that jobless people may have little incentive to take low-paid (or low-hours) employment. As Mead notes, 'making work pay' is very much the vogue in the US at present and New Labour has begun to use the same language in Britain. From a US perspective Mead is rather sceptical about the significance of work disincentives as a cause of joblessness but a brief review of British experience indicates that matters may be more complex than Mead suggests.

Were Mead to examine work incentives in Britain, his *prima facie* conclusion might be the same as that which he draws for the US. Despite constant talk of the very high marginal 'tax' rates (sometime reaching 90 per cent in the £) facing people when they contemplate moving from welfare to work in Britain, it is arguable that work incentives have improved in recent years.

The former Conservative government spent 18 years making benefits for jobless people relatively less generous—with increases in benefit levels pegged to prices rather than earnings—and more closely linked to active job-search (the Jobseeker's Allowance introduced in 1996 represents the culmination of this approach). At the same time the Conservatives placed ever greater stress on the use of in-work benefits to encourage jobless people into low-paid jobs. Over half a million low-paid workers now receive Family Credit (a benefit-based equivalent to the Earned Income Tax Credit Mead describes in the US) at an annual cost of £2 billion.

Unfortunately, the impact of these benefit changes on work incentives has tended to be at least partially offset by other developments. The Wages Councils which set minimum pay rates for around 2.5 million workers in a limited number of industrial sectors were abolished in 1993 and the ability of trade unions to protect the pay and conditions of workers in a wider swathe of industry was reduced by successive items of trade-union legislation. The combined effect of these measures has been to place downward pressure on wage rates which has added momentum to a rise in wage-inequality driven by the shift in demand against unskilled workers described earlier.

'Entry-level' jobs open to people seeking to move from welfare to work nowadays on average pay around £100 per week (roughly a third of the median wage in Britain) which may deter some people from taking jobs.[6] This is one reason why, as part of a broader 'making work pay' strategy, the Labour government will introduce a national minimum wage (albeit it is arguable that, if set at too high a level, any incentives effect of a minimum wage will be offset by its potential to harm job creation). However, in considering work-incentives, it is important to consider entry wages alongside the broader characteristics of jobs open to people on welfare.

The longer people have been unemployed, the more likely they are to enter temporary jobs and thus risk a swift return to benefit; half of all people making fresh claims for unemployment-related benefit in any given quarter have been off benefit for less than a year.[7] Economists disagree about the degree of job insecurity in the British labour market as a whole but it is clear that the lower end of the labour market is a very insecure place to inhabit. One can therefore appreciate why some unemployed people might prefer the relative stability of life on benefit to the prospect of insecure low-paid employment (especially when one considers the difficulty associated with signing on and off benefit within a highly bureaucratised welfare system).

The possibility that some jobless people might prefer to remain on benefit for reasons of income security could also perhaps explain behaviour of the kind Mead describes in the US. Indeed, given that the US labour market exhibits even more 'hire and fire' job flexibility than Britain's, it is perhaps surprising that Mead's analysis of work incentives makes little mention of the stability of jobs on offer to people on welfare other than in a passing reference to the rapid job turnover experienced by some groups.

The desire to maintain income security, notwithstanding the low level of their welfare income, could be said to represent a rational economic response by jobless people in the face of uncertainty. This of course provides an alternative explanation for the behaviour which Mead ascribes to what might be called the negative mind-set of the jobless that prevents them from entering work. Mead's response would presumably be that the same labour market conditions are open to all individuals and therefore that one still needs a sociological or psychological explanation for why some people are less risk-averse, and thus take jobs, than those who do not. However, whilst this is true, before concluding that the risk-averse behaviour of the long-term jobless is psychologically deep-seated, or in some way culturally determined, one should first examine a more obvious possible explanation, i.e. that there is something about the operation of the benefit system itself that alters the behaviour of people on welfare.

Substantive evidence based on international comparisons of countries with different types of labour market and different social systems shows that, when more stress is placed on providing an indefinite welfare safety net to the jobless than on measures to help them into work, spells of unemployment tend to increase.[8] The disadvantage with such a 'welfare strategy' is that by prolonging periods of joblessness it risks making jobless people less employable. This can occur by reducing the motivation and 'job readiness' of the unemployed but equally well by reducing their chances of being hired if employers are reluctant to hire people without an up-to-date work record.

This kind of welfare-based explanation of core joblessness does not depend on any prior assumptions about the causes of a person's joblessness. The initial impetus might be a change in the balance of demand for skills such as was mentioned earlier. But the same outcome can result from macroeconomic instability if the benefit system serves to convert what would otherwise be relatively short bouts of joblessness caused by recessions into prolonged periods without work.

Likewise, short-term unemployment created by ongoing turbulence in product and labour markets—as companies restructure, downsize or introduce new techniques in a continual effort to reduce costs and remain competitive—can also turn into long-term unemployment if policy makers respond to the resulting job insecurity by offering a welfare cushion to the unemployed rather than by helping people to become more mobile from job to job.

The Case For Work Requirements

Viewed in this latter way, the benefit system clearly has the potential to act as a transmission mechanism for long-term joblessness, either by serving to scar the jobless or more generally by limiting their effectiveness as labour market participants. Mead, by contrast, seems to view the benefit system as a misguided means of support for the poor through which public agencies serve to legitimise or 'rubber stamp' the already self-defeating attitudes of the jobless. However, those who prefer the former view to Mead's may nonetheless find that Mead's comments strike a chord of realism about the observed behaviour of people who have lived long-term on welfare, and thus support the general thrust of his case for work requirements.

The current penchant amongst policy makers for 'active' (work-based) over 'passive' (welfare-based) means of help for the jobless—which owes more to the 'employment principle' first adopted by Sweden's Social Democrats than to US workfare—already points to a growing recognition of the dangers inherent in long-term welfare provision to able-bodied people of working age.[9] And within the British context all the main political parties talk—in Kennedyesque terms—of offering the jobless 'a hand-up not a hand-out' (albeit the Liberal Democrats reject the use of mandatory work programmes).

The Conservatives when in power preferred the incentives-based approach to tackling structural unemployment for fear that large-scale work programmes could in effect lead the state into becoming 'employer of last resort' (possibly resulting in what was once described as akin to the 'nationalisation of unemployment'). Yet despite this fear successive Conservative administrations developed the workfare principle by requiring benefit claimants to attend a variety of job-search programmes and in its latter months even moved in the direction of classic workfare in the form of Project Work. This involved offering help with finding jobs to the two-year-plus unemployed followed if necessary by a period of compulsory community work with participants paid their benefit cheque plus £10 per week.

The new Labour government has abandoned Project Work but its New Deal proposals nonetheless indicate that Britain will soon be at the European forefront of the active approach to tackling joblessness. As mentioned earlier, in the case of jobless 18-24-year-olds, tough benefit sanctions will be imposed on people who fail to take advantage of an employment, training or education opportunity. Help under the New Deal will also extend to very long-term unemployed people aged over 25 and jobless single-parents but these latter groups will not be required to join new work or job-search programmes (although if the New Labour fixation on all things American continues at its current pace tougher sanctions on jobless single parents may not be far off).

The Labour government's New Deal can be said to involve a reciprocity of obligations between state and jobless citizen insofar as the responsibility placed on the jobless to come off benefit is to be matched by the provision of new opportunities. In this sense, amongst others, the New Deal differs from the workfare approach as advocated by Mead who is primarily concerned with motivating the jobless to enter available jobs rather than the large scale creation of new temporary job opportunities. Yet there are some practical similarities between Mead's approach and the New Deal.

As well as the benefit sanctions associated with the New Deal, the Labour government, like Mead, stresses the importance of case-management and mentoring for jobless people as they move through work programmes. Given this, perhaps the most direct relevance of Mead's analysis to the current British welfare-to-work debate lies in his observations about what makes work programmes work.

Why does Workfare Work?

Mead defends his case for workfare by arguing that mandatory work programmes are more cost-effective than their voluntary equivalents. On closer examination, however, it would seem that a variety of additional factors also help determine programme success, not least programme design and implementation. In order to answer the question: what works? one thus needs to look inside what Mead describes as 'the black box' of mandatory work programmes in the US.

According to Mead, mandatory programmes are successful because they encourage high participation, give rise to a diversion effect which causes more people to leave welfare of their own accord, and clarify what is expected of welfare claimants. But in addition Mead also points to the importance of work-oriented rather than education- or training-based programmes, detailed case-management and monitoring, and an efficient and committed workfare bureaucracy. What, if any, lessons does this 'package' convey to those currently constructing Britain's New Deal?

Is Compulsion Justified?

Mead's bottom line statement that work programmes must be mandatory is a source of controversy in Britain and is already a cause of underlying concern about the New Deal.[10] The case against compulsory programmes comes in a number of forms. Some argue that, since jobless people want to work, all one needs to do is provide them with worthwhile opportunities and they will come forward voluntarily to take advantage of them. Only if employment programmes are inferior will people need to be forced to participate. Others in addition argue that compulsion can reduce the efficiency of programmes by drawing in reluctant and hence disruptive participants, especially if some of the very hard-core unemployed have underlying psychological traits or problems such as drug-dependency which make them 'difficult customers' to handle.

Mead deals convincingly with the first of these objections by arguing that long-term welfare recipients appear to need a 'push' from public authorities in order to be able to realise their desire for work. His observation that the core jobless have often experienced failure and are fearful to try employment again is at the very heart of the welfare-to-work issue and provides a clear justification for the application of a certain amount of pressure on claimants. In the absence of such pressure only the less fearful and more motivated will be helped, leaving the core problem untouched.

Significantly, however, Mead indicates that heavy-handed use of benefit sanctions can be counterproductive. The purpose of sanctions is to clarify what is expected of the jobless; contrary to the common perception, if used sensitively, sanctions can act as a motivational tool rather than a means of coercion. As Mead states, large-scale application of sanctions suggests failure to exert authority in other ways, implying that work requirements should not be viewed as a form of macho-management of welfare claimants.

One way to establish authority and legitimacy for work programmes in the British context will be to combine sensitive use of the benefit sanctions 'stick' with suitable 'carrots' in the form of quality programme provision. Without this, any work requirement will almost certainly appear punitive and possibly create resentment. Unfortunately, Mead says little about how public authorities in the US deal with people who resent having to participate in programmes, a problem that may prove one of the knottiest for those responsible for enforcing work requirements as part of Britain's New Deal.

The Limits of Diversion

Recalcitrants may, of course, form part of what Mead calls the 'diversionary effect' of workfare, an effect illustrated by the experience of Britain's Project Work scheme. The initial pilot results from Project Work showed that 25 per cent more people left the unemployment register in the pilot areas than in comparable areas. However, only one in ten Project Work participants in the pilot areas are known to have found a job after leaving the programme. The majority simply 'disappeared', though why and to where nobody is quite sure.

Some of those who vanished from the dole queue may have taken jobs in preference to Project Work or 'gone underground' to eke out an existence in some other way, while others may already have been working and claiming benefit fraudulently. Either way Project Work seems to have been more effective as an anti-welfare measure than as a means of helping the genuinely core unemployed into jobs, indicating the limits of the diversion effect *per se* and highlighting the need to ensure that work programmes are effective in a much more rounded way.

The Importance of Programme Design and Implementation

Encouragingly, the Labour government's New Deal programmes seek to do far more than simply divert the jobless off benefit. Mead would no doubt be pleased to discover that the New Deal programmes are primarily work-based, with the required training element being linked to participation in employment. The main exception is that one option available to the 18-24-year-old client group will be up to a year of full-time skills-related education or training. This seems more justified for people from a relatively young age group although it will clearly be important to evaluate the returns to such education or training in terms of improved job entry and earnings.

In the light of Mead's analysis, however, the key to the success of the New Deal may well lie in the effectiveness of case-management. Young jobless people entering the New Deal will first pass through a so-called Gateway where, over a period of four months, they will be assessed, versed in job-search techniques and assigned a case manager who will oversee them during their programme placement and, if necessary, offer help when the placement ends. It is also intended that mentors will be drawn in from the wider community to offer support to case managers.

Responsibility for the Gateway and case-management elements of the New Deal will be given to the Employment Service which will then work in partnership with other public, private and voluntary agencies to ensure delivery of the New Deal programme options. Unfortunately, however, the Employment Service is open to the same kinds of criticism that Mead makes of some existing work and welfare bureaucracies in the US.

One lesson to be drawn from Mead's account is that an innovatory and entrepreneurial zeal is required of public bureaucracies charged with helping the jobless into work. In many instances this can only be established by changing the prevailing bureaucratic culture. Britain's Employment Service has undergone something of a culture change in recent years but further development may be necessary. The Employment Service has, rightly or wrongly, come to be seen as a benefit policeman rather than an agency acting in the best overall interests of the jobless. Within the New Deal the Employment Service will have to combine the carrot and stick with considerable skill and dexterity if it is to exert the right kind of benign authority and meet the government's objectives for reducing structural unemployment.

Conclusion

Whether or not one accepts the conclusions of Professor Mead's analysis of the causes of core joblessness—and it is the contention of this note that in the British context at least the problem can be explained more in terms of barriers to employment than the orientation of the jobless—Mead nonetheless offers some important pointers for Britain's welfare-to-work debate.

Mead's advocacy of a work-based approach to dealing with welfare dependency that is both mandatory and heavy on bureaucracy is obviously controversial. Commentators on the political left will doubtless condemn the 'social authoritarian' aspects of Mead's approach, while those on the right may also object to the creation of a large and potentially intrusive public bureaucracy. A more constructive response, however, would be to listen to what Mead has to say, qualify his conclusions where necessary, but above all to take on board his central message, i.e. that work, not welfare, offers the best hope of improving life for the jobless poor.

Workfare—a Pull, a Push or a Shove?
Balancing Constraint, Opportunity, Compulsion and Autonomy in Individual Experience
Eithne McLaughlin

Introduction

I HAPPENED to be reading Beck's *Risk Society* when Lawrence Mead's paper arrived and I was struck by how the form, as well as the content, of this 'message from America' could be understood as illustrating several of Beck's central themes. Beck[1] comments that class (or modern) societies relate to the ideal of equality (in its various forms from equality of opportunity to equality of outcome) in their developmental dynamics, whereas the normative counter-project of the emerging risk society (or late modernity[2])—'its basis and motive force'—is safety, a perspective that I think illuminates Mead's choice of focus on the [in]competence of those of whom he writes. Further, 'whereas the utopia of equality contains a wealth of substantial and positive goals of social change, the utopia of the risk society remains peculiarly negative and defensive',[3] and it seems to me that Mead's paper has to be read as part of the political and social shift from one utopia to the other that has occurred over the last 15 years or so. This shift is characterised by social crises coming to be viewed more and more as of individual origin and perceived as social only indirectly and to a limited extent,[4] as in Mead's analysis and discourse around the causes of inadequacies in the competencies of poor people.

Contextualising Mead's paper in this way—that is, as reflecting wider processes of change—helped me, at least, to dampen some of the 'noise' in the paper that is otherwise distracting. There is clearly some merit in Mead's paper. He attempts to move debate on from a lot of the nonsense talked in Britain and elsewhere about financial incentives and disincentives being the cause of long-term unemployment. There is also merit in the way he draws attention to the need for high quality assistance and services for long-term unemployed people. Distracting from this, however, is 'noise' that could be crudely summarised as 'every-thing is the parents' (mother's?) fault'. Some of this 'noise' may be caused by the temptation, always present if one wishes to influence policy, to engage in linguistic exaggeration and conceptual over-simplification; a temptation that arises from the competition for public attention. There are, however, also problems with the form of Mead's argument: the use of a great deal of negative evidence makes it difficult to sift the wheat from the chaff. Mead also leaves wide open the question of the degree of 'transference' that is appropriate between two very different countries—different in terms of policy traditions, but also countries which occupy very different places in the world economy.

In what follows, I have chosen not to comment on labour market issues directly, important as these are to the explanation of joblessness and poverty, as these are covered by other contributors. Rather, the lessons the UK can draw from the US experience of programme intervention are examined in the first section of this comment while the second section focuses on what Mead describes as the causes of poverty and unemployment—'[in]competency'—and his argument that the only effective remedy for [in]competency is compulsion.

In brief, I make three main arguments. First, that Mead has not demonstrated that it is compulsion *per se* which accounts for the effectiveness of some US programmes. Second, that Mead's explanation of long-term poverty and joblessness among those of working age in terms of a culture of poverty is not sufficiently substantiated, and that it is simply inadequate to explain the presence of low expectations and reactivity among long-term poor jobless people (that he describes as a problem of 'competency') primarily in terms of weak or abusive parenting. Thirdly, that the 'liberal hesitancy' he notes in relation to the use of compulsion may have a sound basis. There is a potential contradiction involved in intervention aimed at developing and enhancing competence—or capabilities, or the capacity for autonomy—on the one hand, and yet involving restrictions on autonomy (and hence on social and moral development and capacities) on the other, thereby introducing the risk of increasing, rather than reducing, psychological reactivity among those who are the 'targets' of compulsion. This ambivalence cannot be 'wished away', and must instead be carefully taken into account in the design and implementation of interventionist programmes.

The Nature of, and Lessons from, US Programme Interventions

Neither the degree of compulsion used in US programmes, nor whether it is compulsion itself or other things that make good US programmes work, emerge particularly clearly from Mead's paper. For example, it was not clear to me whether the US has had a more mandatory regime in place in relation to benefit recipients than the UK (speaking of the last decade). Comparison is difficult because in the US the targets, or subjects, of active labour market programmes and associated tests of work availability have been lone mothers, not men, whereas the reverse has been the case in the UK.[5] So we must compare what the US has expected of jobless lone mothers with what the UK has required from unemployed men (and a minority of jobless women). How much difference has there been in the extent of compulsion and penalties? The UK has a long history of benefit reductions, and withdrawal, as penalties applied against registered unemployed people for either failing to take up jobs offered or inadequate job-search behaviour (within which, for a decade or more, has been included compulsory attendance at motivation/training courses). In the US 'workfare' has included job-search behaviour and activities as much as work itself. This context is important because those who approach Mead's paper with the belief that the US has been 'tougher' than the UK are probably misguided, and may, therefore, come to inappropriate conclusions about the lessons for the UK.

While the UK has a long tradition of penalising inadequate or insufficient job-search behaviour amongst unemployed benefit recipients, there have been significant differences between the services and programmes available to such recipients in the US and the UK. Clearly, effective US programmes have been more intensive (as typified by the use of case-management) than those to which the majority of UK recipients have been exposed. For readers in the UK, the question will be whether the effectiveness stems from this intensity or from what Mead chooses to emphasise—compulsion. On this point, the evidence Mead provides can be read in several ways. A close reading of Mead's evidence on US programmes seems to me to demonstrate that substantial programme success depended on five things: high quality in the administration of the programme; the multi-faceted nature of programmes; programmes premised on, and practicing, mutual obligation; programmes involving more encouragement than compulsion; and finally, that the more successful a programme is, the more it needs to draw on public sector jobs. These may not be the messages Mead wants to convey but I believe they are messages in the material of the paper itself.

I do not mean to imply that Mead is unaware that it is the quality of the administration, rather than client behaviour, which is the distinguishing factor between successful and unsuccessful programmes. Rather this success seems to be due to several of the factors he identifies, not just (or even) to the mandatory nature of programmes, as he argues. These appear to be: quality of staff; clarity of purpose; and substantial levels of resources invested in administration itself. Wisconsin, for instance, has pumped millions into the administration itself, whereas in the UK over the last decade the Employment Service has been progressively denuded of resources.

In addition, Mead himself acknowledges that it is important for programmes to be multi-aspected. This means arranging appropriate support services (childcare and transport, for instance), and the provision of continued support for, and access to, training and education, after as well as before a movement into work experience or a job. This is very different from the British tradition. Although there is now some recognition of the importance of support services to lone mothers in the new Labour 'welfare-to-work' package, there is considerably less evidence of such a multi-faceted approach in relation to other jobless groups—ironically, precisely the groups in the UK who have obligations to be available for, and search for, work. The importance of a multi-faceted approach is its recognition that in the individual biography there are no boundaries between:

> family and wage labour, education and employment, administration and the transportation system, consumption, pedagogy, and so on. Subsystem boundaries apply to subsystems, not to people in institutionally dependent individual situations.[6]

The emphasis on high-quality and multi-faceted assistance in effective US programmes implies mutual obligation. So scrutiny is rightly directed to the performance of the staff involved in the programme, as well as to the programme parameters: 'everyone involved—staff and contractors as well as clients—is accountable for performance' (p. 45). Recognising that the performance of the programme itself is critical to the success of the endeavour means shifting our gaze away from clients (and their 'inadequacies'), rather than towards them, as Mead asserts. Mutual—that is, reciprocal—obligation is hard to envisage within the confines of the current UK system. I have no doubt that a system based on mutual obligation would bring about an efficiency enhancement. Equally important, however, is the very different message a system based on mutual obligation would send to jobless people in the UK. The 'message' that 'the administration' is required to help them find work is not a message which demoralises and undermines self-respect. What does fatally undermine self-confidence and self-respect is a system where rigorous work enforcement messages are sent, and applied, to jobless benefit recipients, but where those sending the messages have themselves no obligations. And that seems to me to be pretty much the situation that has developed in the UK. To use an example local to me, four-fifths of long-term unemployed people in West Belfast have never been notified of a job vacancy, and nearly three-quarters have never had a job interview arranged for them, by the public employment service.[7] Yet all are required to attend re-motivation courses, apply for a certain number of jobs a week, and collect evidence that they have done so. Mead argues that: 'Work-tests divide the responsibility for overcoming poverty between the government and those who are poor, giving both a role' (p. 51), but I think the UK experience shows that it is not work-tests (i.e. requirements to be available and search for work) themselves which represent joint responsibility. Rather it is effective programmes based on an ethos of mutual obligation which represent such joint responsibility.

Mead emphasises the importance of programmes being mandatory rather than voluntary on the grounds that voluntary programmes in the US have failed. Whether voluntary programmes in either the UK or the US have failed because they are voluntary is difficult to assess (and the term voluntary is used by

Mead in a different way than is the case in the UK). In the UK, the availability of some programmes, particularly those of better quality, has been restricted, so that rather than failing to attract people, they have had to turn them away. In the US, it may be the case that voluntary programmes have been unsuccessful because they have been less well-resourced, less well-staffed, more restricted in scope and less clear of purpose than mandatory programmes. In other words, it is hard to tell whether it is the mandatory nature *per se*, or other factors associated with mandatory programmes, which have produced greater success. Does comparison of more and less successful mandatory programmes shed light on this? Mead notes that:

> at the local level, sanctioning is actually inverse to performance: programme offices that sanction many clients place fewer people in jobs than those that sanction fewer. The reason appears to be that programmes that have to 'throw the book' at non-co-operators have failed to exert authority in more effective and informal ways. Typically, they have failed to make expectations clear to clients up front (p. 33).

In my view sufficient evidence is not available in Mead's paper to determine whether high-sanctioning programmes have this pattern because they have 'failed to exert their authority' and 'make expectations clear to clients up front' (which would support the argument that it is the mandatory nature of the programme which matters), or because they have failed in administrative and performance terms—that is, to offer valuable, worthwhile, assistance to clients, within an ethos of mutual obligation.

As noted above, it is clear that successful programmes in the US practice encouragement more than compulsion. Mead notes that 'little of the welfare savings that programmes generate is due to sanctions; getting people off welfare by other means is far more important' (p. 33), and that '[o]nce involved in the programme, participants themselves chose to take a job more often than they were "forced" to by government' (pp. 25-26). This highlights certain inconsistencies in Mead's argument. His central argument is best represented by the statements that voluntary programmes 'do not reach to the core of the work problem, which is the reluctance of poor adults to take and hold the low-skilled jobs they can already get' (p. 18) and that '[t]he behaviour of seriously poor adults seems to respond more strongly to direction from public authority than it does to economic incentives' (p. 20). Yet the details provided of successful programmes suggest something rather different—a lot less direction and a lot more encouragement than these statements assert or imply. Although Mead describes case-management in effective programmes as 'directive' rule-enforcement (p. 36), the 'direction' involved seems remarkably unauthoritarian, involving strenuous attempts to get people to participate without sanctions:

> When people disappear they pursue them to get them to come back. They call them up, send them letters, go out and visit their homes, if necessary begin proceedings to sanction. In leading programmes, this follow-up is relentless ... At its best, case management combines help and hassle ... Kenosha, for example, had few clients sanctioned but it had many clients in 'reconciliation', a process by which non-co-operators were talked into returning to the programme and thus avoiding sanctions (p. 35).

Just as there is more than one way to skin a cat, so there appears to be more than one way to obtain rule abidance. Nuanced description of what is actually happening in these programmes rather undermines assertions such as the claim that it is the advertising of sanctions—spreading the word '"on the street" that the programme is serious'—rather than the application of the sanctions themselves which 'works' (p. 33). What such intense case-management is likely to be doing is telling the client that there is a realistic probability of success—i.e. the case manager absolutely believes that, if the client will return to participation, successful outcomes can be achieved. It should surprise no-one that the long-term poor and jobless are sufficiently disillusioned and lacking in self-confidence to need to hear this from someone else and to need to hear it more than once—points I will return to in section two.

Mead acknowledges that effective case-management such as that in the most successful US programmes is expensive. But such effective programmes apparently generate another cost as well—because as programmes become more successful, the role of the public sector in providing jobs needs to increase. Although Mead states that '[g]overnment jobs cost much more than simply paying people aid' (p. 21) and that therefore programmes should be directed towards work in the private sector, in the US the solution has not in fact been private sector jobs only: 'To date, most work programmes have been able to place the great majority of clients in the private sector and have needed only a small pool of public positions as a backup for the hard-to-employ' (p. 32). Since, as Mead says, effective mandatory programmes involve higher proportions of long-term welfare recipients than voluntary programmes, the 'hard-to-employ' are present in them in larger numbers, and correspondingly higher ratios of public-to private-sector jobs will be required. Mead, however, seems to continue to assume that the private sector will suffice. Yet, both in regions where the private sector is not currently in a position to absorb large numbers of jobless people, and for the 'hard-to-employ'—those to whom private-sector employers are particularly risk-averse—mandatory work requirements ought to be accompanied by opportunities in the public sector for reasons of fairness. It is clearly unfair to penalise people for not 'taking' jobs in the private sector if they have not been offered jobs in the private sector. Since those doling out the 'punishment' do not have control of the supply of private-sector jobs, unless they are able to offer public-sector opportunities, there will be serious problems of justice in determining how and when punishment should be meted out.

Compulsion and Competence

Mead challenges what he calls the tradition among 'experts' to look for the causes of non-work outside poor people themselves—e.g. low wages, a lack of jobs, childcare demands, racial bias, the benefit system, disability, a lack of marketable skills. He says such explanations appear to 'be a little bit true, but none of them—singly or in combination—appears to explain more than a small part of the work problem' (p. 6). This 'small part' is apparently about a third (p. 11), but with 'the extent varying around the country', though we are given no upper limit to its size. So it may not be that small after all, at least in particular places, even by Mead's own reckoning. The main explanation he believes to be what used to be called 'the culture of poverty' (p. 12) and which Mead now describes as a problem of competency among poor adults. The origins of incompetency, also described by Mead as dysfunction and an inability to act in one's own self-interests, are attributed by Mead to the parents of today's poor adults: 'the ability to cope stems largely from one's family and upbringing. Children are formed in the family, and once they leave it there is remarkably little government can do to change them or to enhance their capacities' (pp. 13-14). He believes that 'the underlying issue is not society so much as the moral responsibility of the poor' (p. 50) and particularly 'the competence one is willing to attribute to poor persons themselves', with conservatives attributing too much competence to them and liberals too little. Mead believes 'the real division [between conservatives and liberals] is over the enforcement of values through public authority' (p. 50).

The Form of the Argument

For me, the first problem in accepting the argument that non-work (and hence long-term working-age poverty) is predominantly caused by something like a 'culture of poverty', pretty much to the exclusion of structural factors, is the form of the argument employed. This can be characterised as 'if X does not prevent the majority from working, then it cannot explain the non-work of a minority'. However, I do not accept that this is either logical or true. Mead presents no direct evidence of the 'reluctance of poor adults to take and hold the low-skilled jobs they can already get' or of the 'culture of poverty' itself. Rather, one possible explanation of poor people's non-work and then another are examined, in each case with evidence produced to show that they are not complete explanations in that they do not explain the work of the majority and hence the non-work of the minority. Mead then concludes that if all these, singly and severally, do not explain non-work, it must be that the poor are reluctant to work for 'cultural' reasons. Quite apart from the logical flaws in this line of reasoning, there is another possibility we must consider. This is that the failure of experts to explain non-work derives from experts not yet being good enough at measuring, understanding and explaining the social and economic worlds. Perhaps we should 'own' our own failures, and not be so ready to assume our 'competence' that we then attribute our failures to the incompetence of others! Such transference may be good for the egos of academics and policy makers, but it adds nothing to the sum of human knowledge. In addition, Mead's argument assumes a realm of culture which is curiously dislocated from everything else, and the problems with this are particularly obvious when Mead sometimes discusses the interactions of culture and structure and at other times rejects such an interaction, a point developed below.

Opportunity and Constraint

Mead's dismissal of racial discrimination as a factor preventing some people from getting jobs is at times expressed rather offensively (for example, p. 8). Yet it is probably true that the size of the discrimination-effect found in the US cannot of itself account for differences in the unemployment and poverty rates between blacks and whites (a situation with parallels in Northern Ireland between the majority and minority populations). This does not, however, mean that discrimination can be summarily discounted, not least because of the effect that knowledge of present (even if relatively small) discrimination has on motivation and expectations. Mead notes that discrimination against minorities is probably worst not for the unemployed but for people in employment (in terms of promotion and white resistance to it (p. 12)), but appears to discount the possibility that this might have any effect on the motivation and expectations of jobless people. On the other hand, he accepts that there has been a historical effect (pp. 12 and 14). Despite his acknowledgment of the effect on 'feelings' of historic lack of opportunities for some groups, Mead concludes: 'My sense is that the opportunity structure has little influence on personal behaviour in the present' (p. 13). Rather, poor people 'project their hopelessness onto the environment but the feeling really arises in the first instance from weak or abusive parenting' (p. 14). So although there is a very real historical connection between the opportunity structure and an individual's attitudes and behaviour, by what can only be regarded as a sleight of hand rather than substantiated argument, this apparently is of no importance in the present—a present which is instead dominated by weak and abusive parenting (for which no evidence is provided, whether of extent or causes).

The result of these parenting deficiencies, Mead argues, is that approaches which assume competence on the part of the individuals to be helped—i.e. that they have 'the capacity at least to advance their own self-interest, if not society's' (p. 13)—are wrong. 'Dysfunction has defeated the preferred opportunity approaches of both left and right' (p. 13) because poor people often do not get through school or work consistently. This, according to Mead, shows that the deep-seated incompetency of poor individuals is caused by weak and abusive parenting, and is not amenable to change by outside forces later in life (p. 14). Logically this means that the long-term working-age poor cannot stop being poor or hold down a job, yet Mead's argument for compulsion and mandatory work programmes is contradictorily premised on the assumption that 'these people' are capable of change—that is, as a result of compulsion, they suddenly acquire a capacity for competence they never had before.

The disillusionment, fragmentation, depression, hopelessness and reactivity among long-term poor people of working age which Mead wishes to focus on are very real phenomena, but they cannot be explained by reference to inadequate parenting alone. What Mead describes as the symptoms of incompetency can also be described as the symptoms of a lack of self-respect, itself the outcome of a biography of restricted autonomy. The failure to develop a sense of, and a capacity for, autonomy is located much more diffusely than Mead allows. Self-respect comes from, and grows or declines with, the respect which others do, or do not, give you, both directly (that is, in interpersonal interactions) and indirectly (that is, through the cultural, social, political and material constructions and experiences of 'people like you'). It is true that abusive parenting is a prime cause of poor self-respect but it is clearly possible for self-respect to languish when one's parents are not abusive. Nor is it the case that the incompetence generated by weak and abusive parenting necessarily leads to long-term poverty. Far more middle-class parents fail their children in terms of the development of self-respect and self-confidence than adults of middle-class origin fall into long-term poverty.

Outside of the realm of family relations, interpersonal interactions with other key adults may involve lack of respect and abusiveness. A good, but not exclusive, example is that of teachers, which Mead himself acknowledges. Mead speaks of the need to restore the authority of parents and mentors (by which he appears to mean primarily teachers) in order to produce competent and masterful young people, yet he notes, in a different context, that authority figures have commonly treated the people who are now poor adults harshly and inconsistently (p. 38), that is, without respect for their humanity and autonomy. Surely the attribution of authority has to be conditional on those involved returning respect for any authority ceded, and this is not something experience suggests we can rely on.

Equally, the material and symbolic circumstances and experiences of one's life can 'teach' a lack of self-respect and create low expectations, in addition to any failures or successes of parenting. For example, quite besides the material effects of living in poverty, growing up in a household on benefits involves confrontation with the judgment of the wider society about how much you are 'worth', a judgment encapsulated in benefit levels. Given the levels of out-of-work benefits, it is impossible to escape the answer, 'not much'. The message that you are not worth much can be reinforced by observing the interactions between your parents (usually your mother) and 'officialdom'. These interactions are framed, and shaped, by the primary task given to 'officials' in the UK—checking and ensuring that your parent's household is abiding by the rules ('their' rules of appropriate behaviour) and not getting anything they do not 'deserve'.

In contrast, it seems to me that Mead individualises the complex interactions between structure and agency, and structure and culture, encapsulated in such experiences. Katz [8] has rightly commented that the search (even competition?) for the relative influence of structure or agency, structure or culture, has revealed more about the methodological preferences of the various academic disciplines than it has about the phenomena they investigate. This comment can probably be applied to individuals within disciplines—that is, that our preferences reveal more about us (not only in terms of our personality structure but also the specific cultural and political sphere within which we work and write), than about the subject under study. I have argued elsewhere that neither the individualisation resorted to by Mead, nor the 'dead hand' of structure resorted to by others, is adequate.[9] We need to examine much more closely how structures of authority, knowledge and power (including those of the social welfare system) set the parameters for individuals' actions, whilst simultaneously investigating the relationships between structures, values and behaviour in individuals' decision-making, and in so doing avoid posing structure against agency, or values/culture against behaviour. We need to understand choice, action, and decision-making as processes over time, and through that understand the interaction between values and beliefs on the one hand and structural and administrative features on the other. This interaction is indeed centrally manifested, as Mead suspects, in expectations.

But it will not do to regard such expectations as formed only in the bosom of the family. Rather they are the result of decision-making environments, which cross-cut family, community, the wider polity and the market. Whilst these environments can change over time, the past as well as the present is always part of each environment. Systems of publicly-funded or subsidised services, within which is included the specific realm of the social welfare system, make a substantial contribution to decision-making environments along three planes. Firstly, in relation to the number of possible courses of action available to different kinds, or groups, of individuals (the quantitative opportunity plane); secondly, in setting the route, or direction, of whatever possible courses of actions there are for the individual (the quality of the opportunity plane); and thirdly, individuals' formulations of the *perceived* probabilities, or likelihoods, of positive outcomes from various possible courses of action (the perceived relationship between formal opportunity and likely outcome). All three planes are experienced simultaneously by the individual, and all involve both past and present policies, and their outcomes. Thus public policy contributes to the shape of individuals' decision-making environments in a number of complex ways—by establishing the parameters of the specific decision-environment for the individual or group of individuals concerned; but also, through its past role in other decision-environments (either directly for the individual concerned or indirectly through the experiences of other individuals with whom this individual identifies, for example, their parents, their peers, their local community), influencing perceptions of the likelihood of positive outcomes (expectations) from the various courses of action possible within these parameters. So when Mead says: 'Parents who would bequeath freedom to their children must first live orderly lives. The source of bondage for today's seriously poor is no longer social injustice but the disorders of their private lives' (p. 15), I am distressed by the lack of attention given to the complexity within which people's expectations form and their daily experiences occur, and, more particularly, the implications of this complexity for the role of public policy in the moral and social development of individuals.

It is not, I think, that Mead is unaware of the frailty of human existence and existing constraints on individual social and moral development. Where he has drawn on information from staff involved in programmes, it is noticeable that the tenor of his discussion changes—some would say 'softens' (see, for example pp. 32-33 and p. 38). It is a disservice to the truth of the overwhelmingly low levels of self-confidence, self-respect and restricted expectations which emerge from even the limited pen portraits thus provided, to suggest that the *solution* must be further restrictions on poor people's autonomy and a political discourse which informs them that the cause of their immiseration is purely personal inadequacy and incompetence. It is for these reasons that I would reject the way Mead sets justice to one side as something unconnected to the issues/problems he discusses (p. 17). Justice may be connected in broader, more diffuse ways with the development of 'competence' through its relationship with self-respect, the capacity for autonomy, and the formation of expectations (see, for example, Wilkinson,[10] in respect of physical and mental health, and Doyal and Gough,[11] more broadly).

Autonomy and Compulsion

Mead criticises liberals because, he says, they would far rather help people work than require them to do so, and both liberals and conservatives, because they 'love to make freedom their instrument, not obligation' (p. 43). Freedom is a word with contested and diverse meanings, but it is not necessarily the opposite of obligation. Autonomy, a more precise conceptualisation which I prefer to 'freedom', is premised on the development of the capacities needed to fulfill obligations to oneself, as well as to others. Autonomy means that people are able 'to formulate consistent aims and strategies which they believe to be in their interests and ... to put them into practice in the activities in which they engage'.[12] The capacities necessary to, or underlying, autonomy are similar to the 'capability of functioning' concept developed by Sen.[13] Doyal and Gough, Sen, and Weale,[14] too, all argue that protecting and ensuring the environmental conditions for the development of capabilities and hence the exercise of autonomy is the overriding justificatory principle for government action. I have argued above that social welfare systems have a complex role to play in bringing into being the conditions in which autonomy can be realised. In the more restricted terms of interventionist programmes targeted at the long-term jobless, the benchmark of success, and the justificatory principle, has to be whether those receiving such intervention experience it as providing for the enhancement or development of capability or the exercise of autonomy, on the one hand, or as restrictive and disabling, on the other. Mead's paper suggests that the best US programmes achieve the former. Thus, clients 'see it as a help ... most recipients ... take it as a form of caring ... to get personal attention of any positive kind is more than many recipients have known. So contact with staff is affirming and the more the better' (p. 38), though I do not think the reasons Mead gives (pp. 37-38) account for this success.

The hesitancy which Mead notes in liberals' approaches to intervention may be founded on good reason. On the one hand, the justification for interventionist programmes lies in the recognition that the capacities fundamental to the exercise of autonomy have not been protected or ensured by government on an equal basis for all in the past, nor are they in the present, and that this is manifest in low expectations[15] and accompanying restricted psychological capacity for proactivity[16] (or competency, capabilities, or autonomy). From a more immediate and restricted perspective, the 'dampening' effects of material poverty, together with the adverse effects of rule-bound existences, on the capacity for proactivity are well-known and indeed described to some extent by Mead (pp. 32-33 and p. 38) and these may justify a mandatory interventionist approach—the initial 'push' as Mead terms it. On the other hand, since the objective of interventionist programmes is to return clients to a state of 'competency', or the capacity for autonomy, there is a valid issue involving the point at which it becomes counterproductive to subject the individuals concerned to (yet more) rules and direction from others, or to lower levels of income (as in the case of benefit penalties or withdrawal). It is this fine line which 'liberal hesitancy', in Mead's terms, 'active labour market policies', in European terms, and 'workfare' programmes, in US terms, have to tread.

Doyal and Gough[17] argue that three variables contribute to autonomy: the level of understanding a person has of themselves, their culture and obligations and expectations; the psychological capacity to formulate their options; and the objective social opportunities to enable them to act. Successful interventionist programmes must enhance all three of these. Neither the first nor the second can be achieved by discourse, practice or analysis founded on 'blaming'. This is why, although persistence is required to assist those who have fallen into reactivity and have little confidence left—to give them at least a starting 'push'—the boundary between persistence and persecution has to be carefully maintained, symbolically as well as in terms of practice.

We cannot 'wish away' the contradictions, and corresponding ambivalence, involved in these issues. Neither are they soluble in any straightforward way. The best that can be achieved is an awareness of the 'fine line' and continual evaluation of interventionist programmes in terms of how well they maintain what is a difficult balance. I will argue below that such evaluation must involve 'clients'' perspectives on the enabling and constraining balance within programmes.

The Rise in Competency Demands

A further justification for a 'push' arises because what Mead calls competency has become more significant as we move towards late modernity/risk society. The reflexive conduct of life, the planning of one's own biography and social relations,[18] makes many more demands on people than was the case in the more prescribed biographies available to most people in even the relatively recent past. The 'simultaneity of individualization and standardization' or the transition from 'standard to elective biography'[19] increasingly characteristic of our times has made people more, not less, dependent on the market, law, education, and so on. The individual 'on pain of permanent disadvantage' must 'conceive of himself or herself as the center of action, as the planning office with respect to his/her own biography, abilities, relationships and so on'.[20] Within this, access to education becomes more critical than in the past—not for the work-relevant qualifications it may or may not produce, but because of its importance in enabling people to forge their own fates, in building capability of functioning, something which 'nobody else can do for me'.[21] The danger with the decrying of education in Mead's paper, in preference for the shorter-term benefits of actually being in a job, is that the latter strategy, if pursued on its own, may mean a continued need for somebody else—the case manager—to 'do it for' the poor. Thus, for both younger and older people, the wider role of education in increasing and facilitating the development of capabilities, competence and the reflexivity upon which proactivity and autonomy are based, must be maintained as a key objective.

Autonomy, Political Expression and Compulsion

I have argued that the balance of interventionist programmes must not swing towards persecution and 'blaming', and that programmes and other public policies must give as much priority to education as to jobs, if the development and enhancement of competence and autonomy are to be the outcomes realised. Such a balance is also desirable in terms of policy efficiency and in the interests of political expression. For instance, Mead's evaluation of US programmes has not involved talking with clients, whether co-operative or recalcitrant (the nearest he has come to this draws on the staff involved in programmes). This is part of a bigger issue about the extent to which an excessive ethos of compulsion can remove the ability of clients to influence prog- ramme review and change by their behaviour and responses to what is on offer. To use the terms developed by Beck,[22] this is a small example of the way reflexivity has been excluded from the social and political interactions between experts and social groups over risks, because of the systematic assumption of realism in science and some parts of the social sciences. The assumption of realism involves the deployment of expert know- ledge as social prescription without any interest or negotiation over its acceptability or validity. Reflexivity necessarily involves negotiation between different epistemologies and subcultural forms and discourses. It is this negotiation which entails the social, moral and political development of the actors involved—in this case, 'experts', policy makers and staff as well as clients. If an excessive ethos of compulsion removes the requirement for such reflexivity, the result is likely to be a reduction in policy efficiency, as experts, policy makers and staff fail to understand what does, and what does not, 'work'. In the case of clients, their responses to the interventions targeted at them can be regarded as forms of informal, pre-political articulations of their semi-private worlds and as a strong vernacular critique.[23] The private reflexivity involved in the generation of such responses is the prior basis for more public forms of participation,[24] and part of, not separate from, the development of autonomy and competence. An excessive ethos of compulsion can, in this sense, inhibit the development of competence, and 'disenfranchise' the poor. Such outcomes would increase the very exclusion and marginality of the poor which is the object of Mead's attentions, and which deserves the attention of us all.

Would Workfare Work?
An Alternative Approach for the UK

Alistair Grimes

U NEMPLOYMENT, AND how we deal with it, remains a central and sensitive issue within western democracies. It is central because, between the end of the Second World War and the 1980s, we assumed low unemployment to be both a political and economic priority. In economic terms, the theories of Keynes in particular seemed to provide a mechanism for maintaining low levels of unemployment and thus maximising the human resources available for economic growth. In political terms, the perceived link between high unemployment, social exclusion, social unrest and, all too frequently, the rise of political extremism, made the maintenance of full employment seem critical to the preservation of democracy itself.

This view started to break down in the United Kingdom during the mid-1970s with the monetarist assault on Keynesian orthodoxy and with the Conservative government after 1979 which clearly placed the control of inflation above that of maintaining full employment. The fact that persistent high unemployment, at levels which might have been thought to produce political instability, did not inhibit the re-election of the Conservatives, served to demonstrate that governments could concentrate on wooing the increasingly affluent middle classes without creating revolution and, worse still, electoral annihilation.

But the fact that the political and economic rule book has been rewritten to include the possibility of reasonable economic growth, stable and low inflation, increased affluence overall and yet have levels of unemployment that would have seemed unacceptable 25 years ago, leaves policy makers with a number of dilemmas. Do they continue to espouse the cause of full employment in the sense in which it existed in the 1950s and

97

1960s? In which case how exactly do they plan to deliver it when any conceivable level of sustainable growth in the UK is unlikely to reduce it below one million? Or do they accept that keeping unemployment at around 1.25 million is as good as it is going to get? In which case what are the plans for this conscript army of cannon fodder in the war against inflation? It will certainly be a test of the Blair government's rhetoric on 'one nation socialism' since, whilst there is no reason for a market to find useful activity for everyone, there is every reason for a society to ensure that all its members are both contributing and cared for.

This brings us on to the issue of sensitivity. With full employment, the market operated in such a way as to find jobs for almost all who wanted one. Those who were deliberately avoiding work in order to draw benefits (and possibly participate in the black market at the same time) were so insignificant numerically as to be unimportant and could be rooted out through procedures designed to detect fraud within the benefits system. But with higher levels of unemployment, and with high levels of long-term unemployment (understood here to be twelve months or more) the issues of cost to the public purse and the relationship between benefits and activities, rights and responsibilities, becomes more pressing. If we accept the pragmatic argument that prolonged periods of inactivity are likely to inhibit people from returning to the labour market, or if we accept as a matter of principle that support from the state demands a reciprocal contribution from the individual, what policies should we pursue?

Why should this be sensitive? Different countries will have different reasons. If I read Mead correctly, for example, in the USA the issue is sensitive partly because of the racial dimension to unemployment. In the UK it is sensitive on the liberal left because it conflicts with the view that the vast majority of the unemployed want a job and cannot get one, not because of their own indolence, but because of lack of demand in the economy, which is itself the result of government macro-economic policies. But part of the reason for the sensitivity of the issue and the confusion which often accompanies the debate is also the strong ideological flavour attached to the various positions. The term 'workfare', for example, rather than being seen as a complex range of different options including versions on offer in Sweden as well as California, becomes (on the left) a shorthand way of accusing political opponents of wishing to force the unemployed, who have no realistic chance of getting a job, into some cosmetic activity for punitive rather than practical reasons. At the other end of the political spectrum, those on the right see opposition to some form of activity in return for state support as a symptom of a 1960s 'something-for-nothing' culture which will eventually undermine any kind of standards and lead to the destruction of society.

I believe that Mead has done the debate a great service by clearly defining his view of what workfare is and by giving a coherent set of arguments to support his view. What I want to do in the rest of this contribution is to restate (accurately I hope) what I take to be the core of those views, to indicate where I agree with them and to explore some of the areas where I believe him to be misconceived, or where I believe his views are not relevant to the position in the UK, no matter how pertinent they are to the situation in the USA. In this last section I will draw on my own experience of being involved in programmes to help long-term unemployed people into work over the last 14 years and, in particular, on my experience of a number of voluntary programmes in Glasgow, most notably Glasgow Works and the Wise Group.

Mead's starting point is that the main cause of poverty is the low level of work amongst the poor. Why should this be the case? Why do poor adults work so much less consistently than better-off adults? According to Mead, conventional solutions have tended to search for impediments outside of poor people themselves such as low wages, lack of childcare, the sheer lack of jobs, racial bias, disincentives in the welfare system, disability or the lack of marketable skills. His reply is that all of these views contain a little bit of truth, but none of them offers a convincing overall explanation either on their own or in combination (p. 6). This is not to say that barriers of the kind mentioned above are unimportant. Mead estimates that about a third of the work problem amongst the seriously poor might be attributable to limits of opportunity in all forms (p. 11) but he goes on to argue that a more important factor is what used to be called the culture of poverty (p. 12). In short, the poor do need to take some of the blame. Many poor adults do not take up jobs that are available to them, resulting in an underclass which is re-inforced in the inner-city ghetto areas because values surrounding the need to work have exited along with the middle classes who used to uphold them. Given the loss of these values over a number of years, programmes designed to promote opportunity will fail simply because most of the individuals at whom they are aimed are too dysfunctional to take advantage of them. To this extent, a lot of preparatory work will need to be done to create any sort of base on which opportunity programmes can build. Amongst these areas for action are restoring basic law and order in the cities, helping to rebuild the family unit and requiring that poor parents work. This last point is not to punish them, but to restore their ability to function in a social world and to prepare them for the world of work. For Mead, liberation from poverty is inextricably bound up with obligation and the sense of discipline it instils.

Central to Mead's argument is his contention that, in the USA at least, voluntary work programmes have failed (or where they have succeeded they have been prohibitively expensive) and compulsory programmes in a number of very different states have been markedly more successful. It is not, of course, compulsion alone, and Mead makes the point that good supervision and support in these programmes are crucial to getting the unemployed back to work. In this sense there is an element of paternalism in the Mead approach, which he would argue is no bad thing if contrasted with the condescension of liberals and the hostility of new-right conservatives. Mead's view is that dependency cannot be abolished in the short run, but it can be made less passive, as the prelude to rebuilding those values of personal effort which, allied to government support, can produce long-term sustainable improvements (p. 51).

It is difficult to disagree with Mead in a number of areas. Let us deal with the issue of principle first. Should taxpayers expect people to contribute activity in return for state benefits? My own view is that this is unexceptionable, provided a number of conditions are met. The first concerns those who are unable to work, either by virtue of illness, injury, or other exceptional circumstances. There is nothing in Mead to suggest that he would not agree with this. As we have seen, his view is not a punitive one. The judgement of who fits into this category is often a difficult one at the practical level and will be discussed below. The second concerns the quality of the programmes on offer to those who are compelled to take them up. Rights and responsibilities need to be balanced around a notion of fairness here, as would be the case in any implicit contract. The consent of the governed is necessary if the law is not to fall into disrepute. But we should also note that accepting the principle of compulsion does not mean that it should be applied, in practice, as the first resort.

At the practical level I think that Mead is correct to stress a number of features. In particular I agree with his view that peer group pressure is an important factor, whether it is a negative one within the culture-of-poverty hypothesis[1] or a positive one in the context of a particular programme. As he recognises, one cannot underestimate the importance of having good staff dealing directly with unemployed people, whether they be trainers, supervisors or counsellors.

But there is little point in writing out a long (or short) list of areas where I agree with Mead, and I want to turn to some of the areas where I disagree with him, or find him less than convincing.

One issue worth raising at this point is the purpose of compulsory programmes. Mead sometimes talks as if the objective is to get people into jobs, but at other times he slips into talking as if the objective is to get them to leave welfare. I think his primary purpose is the former, but the distinction is an important one, especially in the context of the current British debate where a similar ambiguity exists. A good example of this was to be found in the Conservative government's Project Work programme. As the name implies, the initial aim was described as that of helping those who had been out of work for two years or more into jobs through a compulsory work-experience programme. The programme failed to achieve this to any significant degree, with about eight per cent of participants getting a job, but did result in large numbers of beneficiaries (up to 25 per cent in some areas) leaving the unemployment register. It was this latter achievement which then became the new aim of the programme. My own view is that if a compulsory programme is to have any credibility with unemployed people and the general public, it must be an into-work rather than a leaving-welfare programme. This brings us back to the issue of judging those who are genuinely not capable of working and therefore exempt from sanctions. If those administering the programme are trying to help those capable of work back into a job, then they are likely to take a more generous view of incapacity, since there is little virtue in sending people on a programme that they cannot ultimately benefit from. If on the other hand the objective is to remove people from the welfare system and save money, they are likely to take a less generous view since the application of sanctions is more likely to achieve that end.

A second general issue is, of course, that compulsion implies the existence of sanctions. But it is not clear from Mead what the level and duration of those sanctions should be, and what element of discretion should be available. Again, in the British context this is an important practical consideration for the new government. Should benefits be withdrawn permanently, or on another basis?

This brings us to a much more fundamental area of disagreement. I am not convinced that, in the UK at least, voluntary programmes have failed, and that compulsion is, therefore, required. Indeed, I believe that to introduce the psychology and terminology of compulsion into the UK at this point in time will undermine the credibility of a number of successful programmes with unemployed people and re-inforce a number of negative perceptions about training, in particular, which are detrimental to another part of the government's programme around lifetime learning and improved standards within the British workforce.

Moreover, introducing compulsion undermines a very important source of consumer feedback on the attractiveness of such programmes, namely the ability to reject them, not out of idleness, but because they are of poor quality. If the present government believes that consumer choice and competition improve quality, since those who produce goods that no-one wants, or can get cheaper elsewhere, go out of business, then it is surely odd to introduce a programme within which there is no effective consumer choice at all and expect anything other than standards clustering at the minimum acceptable level rather than improving in response to market signals.

Let me start this defence of voluntary programmes by making some observations about unemployment and unemployed people in the UK. The unemployed are not an homogenous set with a universal solution which will suit them all. We need to start by considering their various needs, aspirations and requirements. The ease with which people have been recruited to good quality training and work-experience in Glasgow over the last 14 years indicates that, for a considerable number of unemployed people, there is an overwhelming desire to work. Some families and individuals do, no doubt, fall into Mead's culture-of-poverty category, but the evidence is that this is still a minority, often concentrated in certain areas of the city. A second point is that many unemployed people, especially young people, have had a less than inspiring experience within the educational system and, sadly, see training as 'school for adults'. Their overwhelming perception, born of participating in several government schemes, is that training is a punishment for being out of work rather than an activity which will help them to improve their chances of employment. Compulsion will merely reinforce this perception. There is a further danger that, if the balance in a group of trainees is tipped towards a majority of them being conscripts, then the peer group pressure will undermine the attempts of those who do want to learn, rather than the other way around.

Programmes which have been able to base their activities on an understanding of what unemployed people want have, in fact, been both successful and cost-effective. The first organisation to develop this in Glasgow was the Wise Group, but it is interesting to note that Glasgow Works has been able to replicate (and in some areas improve on) these results and that clones or franchises of this model (known somewhat inelegantly as the Intermediate Labour Market [ILM]) have achieved similar levels of success in London, Motherwell, Sunderland and Derby.

What is the evidence? The Wise Group has been evaluated by Glasgow University on behalf of the Rowntree Foundation[2] and Glasgow Works has been evaluated by Cambridge Policy Consultants (formerly PACEC) on behalf of Scottish Enterprise and the Scottish Office.[3]

Both evaluations have considerable similarities. In the case of the Wise Group 67 per cent of trainees had had a job at some point within six months after leaving the programme and, measured at three and six months after leaving the programme, some 45 per cent of trainees were still in work. This compares

with a figure of 23.9 per cent for the main government programme for the long-term unemployed in Glasgow, Training for
Work (TfW). The figures for Glasgow Works are virtually identical,
indicating that ILMs are nearly three times as effective. What is
more impressive is the fact that over 80 per cent of ILM trainees
have been out of work for a year, and 33 per cent for two years,
compared with TfW where only 55 per cent of trainees have been
out of work for a year or more—in short, better results with a
more difficult client group. Glasgow Works has had a control
group of unemployed trainees on TfW, matched for length of
unemployment, gender and so on. This group only achieved a 20
per cent success rate into jobs, compared with a figure of 66 per
cent for Glasgow Workers. In the case of the Wise Group, one
other interesting feature is that even amongst those who have
been out of work for two years, 44 per cent were still getting a
job.

The fact that a significant number of trainees were still in the
same job, or had moved to another job, reinforces the view that
the key to moving up in the labour market is having a job
already, and that even starting at the bottom is a useful stepping
stone. Mead would, I think, agree with this. Indeed it is part of
his argument for forcing people to work that it prevents them
passing up such potential opportunities to get a foot on the
ladder.

It would, however, be a mistake to assume that jobs for ILM
participants when they leave the programme are all low-quality
or low-paid. In the case of Wise Group trainees, some 61 per cent
of jobs were full-time, increasing to 67 per cent amongst those
still in a job after six months, with the vast majority being
permanent rather than temporary contracts. In terms of wages,
only 19 per cent were taking home less than the amount they
were receiving under the Wise Group programme (£100 per week)
and over 36 per cent were taking home more than £150 per
week, a figure which increased to 53 per cent amongst those who
had moved to a second job after leaving the Wise Group.

If these evaluations are in any way accurate, then ILMs seem
to produce a considerably higher proportion of positive outputs
than government programmes, with a more difficult client group,
and the outputs appear to be sustained, placing long-term
unemployed people into jobs that are, in terms of the local labour

market, well paid for the level of skills and qualifications. Why should this be the case?

An ILM is based on the idea that unemployed people do want to work, but have often lost the disciplines and patterns of work behaviour or, in the case of young people, never really acquired them. The programme is, therefore, as much like work as possible in the sense that the trainees carry out activities which produce goods and services that are of value to their local communities such as energy conservation and advice, security, environmental improvements, recycling or care services. Interestingly, none of these areas produce serious displacement of private sector activity. This is underpinned by paying a wage (after an initial eight-week trial period) which reinforces the idea that this is not a make-work scheme and that people are expected to behave like employees, with an acceptance of the disciplines of work which go alongside this. As Mead notes in another context, good supervision and support are critical and pay off. Trainees are on the programme for a maximum of twelve months, time enough to allow them to readjust to the world of work without making it a permanent job, so they still have to find future employment.

The other benefit of the ILM is that it meets the employer's need to find potential employees who are 'work ready' and have demonstrated that they have the necessary 'softer' skills to hold down a job. One of the paradoxes of government training programmes is that by sending people to a training course they only lengthen, in the employers mind, the perceived period of unemployment.

One objection to ILMs is that they are expensive. There is an element of truth in this, given that the cost of a place in the Wise Group is around £14,000 per year and in Glasgow Works around £12,500. However, on a value for money basis they compare very favourably with the alternatives. Even acknowledging that TfW is cheaper per person, once the better rate of getting people into jobs is taken into account, Glasgow Works is still cheaper than TfW (this calculation is not available for the Wise Group). And none of these calculations take into account the savings or additional benefits from the goods or services produced by ILM trainees.

It may also be worth adding that we should not be surprised that dealing with long-term unemployment is expensive. Given that a large number of 'dysfunctional' individuals and families are involved, it is surely unreasonable to expect a quick and cheap solution to be available. Searching for a cheap, as opposed to a cost-effective, solution will not produce the desired results. The argument is surely that an investment in solving, or at least reducing, the problem will pay off in the long-term by reducing the flow of people into long-term unemployment and reducing the stock to manageable proportions over time.

Both Glasgow Works and the Wise Group demonstrate that voluntary programmes, if they are of high quality and meet the basic desire of the unemployed person to earn a wage, can deliver results. The problem which has bedevilled so many UK programmes which have failed the unemployed has not been the psychology of the unemployed but the poor quality of the programmes on offer. As we have noted above, compulsion removes the ability of consumers to vote with their feet, so the alternative to ensuring quality must, therefore, reside in the ability of those administering programmes to police them effectively.

The thrust of my argument so far is that compulsion, whatever the issue of principle, is in practical terms unnecessary in the UK. There would be plenty of takers for a quality programme which gave people a realistic hope of getting a job and was not seen as a low-cost 'parking place' for the unemployed who will then be returned to the dole queue for another six months before requalifying for their next stint on workfare. In this respect the UK may be different from the rest of Europe in that the relatively low level of benefits compared to wages still makes it possible for most unemployed people to be better off in work.

I want to end by considering two further potentially damaging side-effects of compulsion. I have already suggested that compulsion should not be necessary, but it is also worth considering whether or not it is practical in a way that is consistent with the commitment to quality which Mead and I share. Whatever the case in the USA, I have severe doubts as to the existence of sufficient capacity at the required level within the UK to deliver the objectives of workfare in Mead's sense. Now this may be an argument for building up to workfare in an incremental way, rather than launching a 'big bang' programme, but at the very least the UK would require a significant investment in, and a reasonable timescale to put in place, the local capacity required. An analogy is with transport, where someone might decide that it would be a good thing if everyone in London went to work on a bus instead of in their car, but omits to build enough buses to satisfy the new demand and then compounds the problem by making bus travel compulsory and penalising people for not travelling that way, no matter how run-down and overcrowded the buses may be.

Second, I want to re-emphasise the damaging effects of having the desire of voluntary participants swamped by those who are there because they have to be. The balance in a group of unemployed people is important. Ten keen trainees can help to turn around the attitudes of four or five who are not so keen, but when the balance approaches 50-50 the sad fact is that it is often those who are not keen who influence the others.

To conclude: both Mead and I agree that getting poor people into jobs is the best way to get them out of poverty and to give them a sense of worth and self-esteem. Mead wishes that this might be done on a voluntary basis, but fears that in the USA the damage of successive generations of inept policies, racism and other factors now make this impossible:

> The poor must be required to work, not just offered the chance to ... because of the nature of the poverty problem and our failure to solve it on a voluntary basis (p. 2).

I do not believe that this situation pertains in the UK. We should not reject the chance to solve the problem here on the basis of voluntary participation and in doing so to ensure that a number of practical benefits accrue and a number of practical defects in compulsory programmes do not occur. For once, there is an alternative.

From Welfare to Work— and Back Again?

Dee Cook

Introduction

LAWRENCE MEAD'S article tells us three things:

- firstly, that the main reason for poverty is *lack of regular work* (p. 1);
- secondly, that in terms of combatting low work levels amongst the poor *workfare 'delivers the goods'* (p. 41);
- thirdly, there is 'no alternative' to the workfare strategy (p. 51).

This commentary will both explore and challenge these assertions by raising some very basic questions about the nature, scope and quality of this argument. Ultimately, I will argue that:

- the relationships between work levels and poverty which Mead poses are both simplistic and distorted;
- that there is little evidence that workfare 'works', particularly in the longer term;
- and that in the UK context there are indeed alternatives which are potentially more workable and more fair than the US model he offers.

What is the problem?

The nature of the problem Mead is addressing is captured in the title of his first chapter—'Poverty and the Failure to Work'. It is not that the poor *can't work*, but that they *won't work*. Consequently, he states that chronic poverty persists in the USA not because the poor lack the opportunity to work, but because we expect too little of them. Therefore, to effectively tackle this chronic poverty, we should expect (and require) the poor to work for their welfare. This expectation is to be enforced and sanctions applied to those who do not comply. In this way, he argues, mandatory work programmes will restore both the work ethic and work levels amongst the poor in a way which voluntary programmes have failed to do.

In a glaringly obvious argument we are told that:

> Many fewer adults work regularly among the poor than the better-off, and... lack of employment is the main reason people are poor today (p. viii).

Of course more of the better-off work regularly—that is precisely why they are better off! But as for the poor, Mead's circular argument is suggesting that people are poor because they do not (want to) work—and the reason they do not want to work is because they are poor. If the central problem—poverty—is caused by low work levels, then the answer for Mead is to raise those work levels by compulsory workfare.

But the distinct issues of poverty and un(der)employment are being conflated here: they are being seen as both cause and effect of one another. Although flawed, the simplicity of his argument does seem powerful at first, until we are asked to accept that it is *individuals* who are responsible for their own low work levels and, consequently, for their own poverty:

> [f]ew poor adults work regularly. That is the main reason they are poor, and it is difficult to trace the problem to limitations of opportunity, such as low wages or lack of jobs (p. 1).

Although no empirical evidence is presented to back up this 'broad brush' assertion, we are asked to accept that there are abundant jobs available for the poor, if only they would take them. To support the assertion that plentiful jobs are available ('at some legal wage', anyway), Mead notes that '[t]he continuing influx of foreign immigrants, both legal and illegal, into the US is just one proof of this' (p. 9). At this point the waters become muddied: whether legal wages or not, whether legal or illegal employees, seems not to matter in this argument. This is reminiscent of Margaret Thatcher's response to a burgeoning hidden economy: even though the activities of legitimate traders and workers were being undercut, she triumphantly asserted that it showed that 'the enterprise is still there!'[1]

Having argued that the poor are poor because of their failure to work, Mead goes on to assert that significant numbers of the poor *are* indeed working, but that this work is often in the hidden economy—that they are employed, illegally, 'on the side', while claiming benefits (p. 3). If we accept this assertion, then the problem of poverty and welfare dependency is *not* one of idleness and low work levels at all: the problem is that the poor are making the rational economic calculation that the wages paid in the kinds of jobs on offer to them are insufficient to maintain themselves and their families. For Mead, however, the answer is for the poor simply to work more and more hours until the wages earned make it worth their while to leave the welfare rolls— notwithstanding, of course, any problems they may experience around family support and childcare arrangements.

In addition to the problem of low pay, lack of domestic and childcare support can prove a key stumbling block to lone mothers and carers moving from welfare to work. But these very real problems are dismissed in Mead's discussion of work levels amongst lone mothers on welfare: '[w]elfare mothers are needy mainly because of low working hours, not low wages' (p. 3) and consequently '[i]t is valid to say that mothers cannot work off welfare without higher wages only if we accept their current low hours as given' (p. 7). So, they should just work longer hours— regardless of responsibilities to those in their care and regardless of the level of wages on offer!

From the discussion so far we can see that the 'problem' which workfare is addressing can be seen in two very different ways. Firstly, according to Mead, the problem is that the poor will not undertake the jobs which are available to them and are *unwilling* to work long enough hours to make these jobs 'pay'. According to the second perspective, the poor simply *cannot afford* to take the kinds of jobs which are on offer to them. Ironically, benefit claimants who engage in fraud by working while claiming serve to justify the imagery of the undeserving 'scrounger' which, in turn, undercuts public and political support for welfare provision for the able-bodied poor. And, in a neat closure of this self-fulfilling argument, lack of popular support for such claimant groups is cited as a crucial justification for establishing workfare programmes in the first place!

It is very significant that any explanation for poverty in terms of low pay is completely denied by Mead: contrary to all the evidence available in the UK context[2] he argues that '[p]overty ...

has little connection to low wages in general' (p. 7). But, on the contrary, recent UK research evidences both the scale of the problem of low pay and the additional difficulties it poses for those attempting to go from welfare into work. In 1996 half of all British employees earned below the Council of Europe's decency threshold (at 68 per cent of average earnings) and people leaving unemployment were being paid an average of only £100 per week, a drop of 12 per cent in real terms since 1980.[3]

Low pay clearly represents a financial obstacle to the poor moving from welfare to work. This obstacle cannot be removed by a workfare strategy which is rooted in compulsion and defies this basic economic logic—that individuals cannot reasonably be expected to *worsen* their already poor living standards by entering full-time regular work! As I will go on to argue below, the structural problems of casualisation and low pay which are associated with a 'flexible' labour market must be addressed as a first priority if positive work incentives are to be offered and poverty is to be effectively tackled.

'Who' Is The Problem?

At this point it is important to remind ourselves that the argument presented here for workfare is not just an economic one—it has individual and moral dimensions too. It is also about problem individuals in problem families in problem localities:

> In the urban setting, these poor people primarily mean long-term welfare mothers and low skilled single men, who are often the absent fathers of welfare families (p. 2).

Thus the lone mothers and fatherless families which allegedly characterise the underclass are central to Mead's understanding of both the causes and the characteristics of poverty itself. Once again, cause and effect are confused: lone mothers on welfare are not only symptoms of the underclass, but they are held to explain its origins too.

Drawing heavily on Murray's notions of underclass,[4] the way in which this workless urban underclass is conceptualised in Mead's argument is not only gendered but is racialised too, for example, in the way in which he appears to accept uncritically the assertion by some businessmen that they are reluctant to hire from the inner city because they 'typically have found unskilled black workers, especially men, to be unreliable' (p. 8). The complex interaction of factors ranging from education and employment history, locality and discrimination, are all undercut by such crude stereotypes. While accepting the 'historic lack of opportunity that minority groups ... knew ... in the past' (p. 12), Mead uses this to account for a racialised culture of poverty within which causes some to feel 'unconvinced that it is worth striving in America, despite the equal opportunity reforms of recent decades. This element has given rise to much of the underclass' (p. 12).

The connections between 'race' and the underclass are further fused in the way in which Mead uses the concept of the 'ghetto'. He sees the ghetto characterised by a pathological culture which has a life of its own and persists independent of the broader society and the ups and downs of the economy. Here, within the ghetto, the poor—and poor 'blacks'[sic] in particular—are seen as being in a world of their own because: '[t]he problems of the ghetto, including non-work, are much the same in good times and bad' (p. 11). If we accept this argument, why bother at all with workfare or indeed any other effort to combat non-work and poverty?

At this point it is worth asking ourselves exactly what is the problem which workfare (and this article) is seeking to address? At its conclusion, Mead refers to the need for a solution to 'the inner city' itself, and his comments on black politicians seem to similarly problematise the issue of 'race', rather than the problem of poverty to which workfare programmes (and the article) are ostensibly directed (p. 51).

But, once again, worrying paradoxes are evident: we are told that if poor adults are to 'make it' in the labour market, 'these Americans have to display something more like the tenacity in seeking and retaining work that immigrants to this country often do' (p. 18). Expressing sentiments which, in an academic or policy context, would seem to me to beggar belief, Mead seems to be saying that if only all the poor worked as hard as 'immigrants', workfare would be unnecessary!

Where the long-term poor are concerned—notably minority ethnic groups, fatherless families and lone mothers—the central feature of Mead's argument is 'victim-blaming'. While acknowledging that some barriers to work (in terms of discrimination and lack of opportunity) do exist, he dismisses the extent of their impact: '[m]y judgement is that about a third of the work problem among the seriously poor might be attributable to limits to opportunity in all forms' (p. 11). What about the other two-thirds? Are we to assume that this is the fault of the poor themselves? There is no indication of how this one-third and two-third attribution of blame for poverty is arrived at, but Mead goes on to spell out more clearly who is at fault and why: 'need usually results in the first instance from self-defeating actions by poor people themselves, particularly non-work, unwed childbearing, and crime ... the ability to cope stems largely from one's family and upbringing' (p. 13).

Here, in a nutshell, are the characteristics of the underclass - lone motherhood, 'problem' families, unemployment, poverty and crime. What is absent is any acknowledgement of the complexity of the relationships between these factors. Mead therefore wrongly assumes a simplistic, linear and causal link between family/unemployment/poverty/crime which may be echoed by media pundits, politicians and publicans alike, but is not supported by academic research evidence.[5]

Once again the focus of the problem which this paper on workfare programmes is addressing has shifted—from the economic and social to the individual level. The problem of disordered lives generates social disorder and so, Mead argues:

> The main task of social policy is no longer to reform society but to restore the authority of parents and other mentors who shape citizens ... the best single thing [government] can do is to restore order in the inner city. Above all, it can require that poor parents work because employment failures are the greatest cause of family failures (p. 15).

This is not to say that Mead would not like to see policies address 'problems' such as 'unwed childbearing', but he laments that:

> nobody has found one that clearly works. We know something about how to enforce work, but almost nothing about how to confine pregnancy to marriage (p. 43).

The Element of Compulsion: The Case of Lone Mothers

Mead describes the history of a variety of enforced work and training programmes: controversially, welfare mothers have increasingly been targeted by such programmes. The 1996 PWORA welfare law requires all adults to work within two years of claiming, though states may exempt mothers with children 'under one year' (p. 24). In the contemporary UK context, the new Labour government's 'New Deal' for lone mothers stresses 'empowerment' and encouragement to work, whereas the model from the US stresses compulsion and enforcement. The motivation in the latter seems clear: 'reducing dependency' (p. 24) and achieving 'a clear profit for government' (p. 25). Although the same motives could be attributed to New Labour, the means by which the welfare dependency of, and welfare spending on, lone mothers is to be reduced does differ considerably.[6]

The element of compulsion evident in the US workfare model has continued to operate in the case of lone mothers, irrespective of the 'barriers' of appropriate work and the availability of childcare facilities. Nonetheless, we are told that '[l]ack of jobs or childcare has not been a major impediment in most localities' (p. 24). It is, however, unclear *who* has performed the childcare role for mothers compelled to undertake workfare programmes. We could assume that either the 'family' and other informal networks have taken the slack, or that the quality of childcare which lone mothers can access is not an issue which concerns the workfare enforcers—or we could assume both. Childcare support is not an aspect which seems to concern proponents of workfare programmes for lone mothers: the enforcement of the programme itself is the paramount concern.

More fundamentally still, Mead does not address the issue of why (and whether) it should be mandatory for mothers of young children to be compelled to work (or train) in return for state support for themselves and their children. Ironically, Mead earlier argued that social order in general, and the individual's ability to cope in particular, stemmed from the family: it is, therefore difficult to see how adding to family stress (through enforced workfare for lone mothers) could be productive in any way—other than for the state, by deterring and reducing its welfare expenditure. (This point is developed further by Melanie Phillips in her essay in this book).

'Help and Hassle'

Mead tells us that 'effective work programmes must be highly prescriptive and authoritative' (p. 26). The watchword here is 'authoritative', as he goes on to describe going on welfare as being 'like going into the army. Those who qualify receive undoubted financial support and other benefits, but in return they have to function in clear-cut ways' (p. 26). The punitive and regulatory aspects of work programmes are seen as central to its (alleged) success. After all, they are dealing with individuals who lack the drive and will to 'make it':

> Most adults on welfare would like to work in principle, but they are pre-occupied with day-to-day survival. Few will make the initial effort to organise themselves for regular activity outside the home unless it is required. Entry into work or job-search must also be enforced (pp. 32-33).

But for the poor, compulsion and enforcement is given a familiar spin—it is for their own good. Although the programme directors Mead quotes admit to being 'all over every client like flypaper! Every day', this form of case-management is rendered benign if it is seen, rather, as just a combination of 'help and hassle' (p. 35).

There is no such thing as too much contact and monitoring of clients because 'it reminds them that you *care*, and that you're *watching*' (p. 38). The image of Foucault's carceral network and the disciplinary power of perpetual surveillance all spring from these quotations![7]

There is no doubt that workfare programmes are essentially punitive in character: they demand compliance and are supported by sanctions. In this sense the dividing line between hard (formal) and soft (welfare) policing begins to blur—both in theory and in practice—as the poor find themselves under perpetual surveillance and also liable to financial penalties for rule-breaking. In this way (and to use the metaphor formerly applied to the increasingly punitive role of probation officers in the UK), workfare programme directors may similarly be seen as 'screws on wheels', as welfare punishment in the community extends to the 'case-management' of the lives of the poor.

The enforcement and monitoring of work programmes described by Mead is labour-intensive and involves complex feedback and management information systems (p. 36). Mead admits that work enforcement makes great demands on state and agency bureaucracies. So, just as crime control has become an industry,[8] so US workfare has become one too. The problem here is the profit motive—for both state and workfare agency

—which may subvert the more humane 'empowering' intentions within work programmes. At the same time, the desire to show a profit (in terms of agency or state welfare accounts) is bound to distort evaluations of how effective workfare really is—and this brings us on to the next crucial question ...

Does Workfare 'Deliver the Goods'?

Mead's assertion that mandatory workfare programmes 'deliver the goods' (p. 41) can only be tested if we are clear about exactly what the goods are that it is said to deliver: in other words, we can only see how successful workfare actually is if we know exactly how its effectiveness is being measured. This is not as easy as it sounds. What is success, in workfare terms? At various points in this article success is taken to mean the adult poor moving on to:

- full-time, regular paid work
- 'steady' work
- part-time work
- unpaid work
- undertaking job-search activities
- undertaking training programmes
- successfully completing education or training programmes
- 'self-improvement'

Clearly, not all of these options are equally valuable (or equally enduring) from the individual's point of view. But they do mark success for the state or the workfare agency if the adult poor are removed from the welfare rolls. So, it could be argued that workfare delivers the good only if those goods are reductions in welfare caseloads (and, hence, welfare expenditure).

But cost-cutting is not the only possible measure of success for workfare: the element of deterrence is also crucial. The regulatory and policing aspects of workfare programmes can be seen as a deliberate attempt to deter welfare claims from the adult poor (especially lone mothers). To this extent, the cost of such programmes is not necessarily uppermost if their aim is predominantly moral—to enforce family norms, instil individual discipline or promote social order.

When it comes to assessing whether workfare works, key questions about the aims of such programmes remain unanswered by Mead. But, to return to the beginning of his argument, if the poor are poor for two reasons: (1) because they are disconnected from the world of work and (2) because they do not work sufficient hours to 'work off' welfare, which set of problems are workfare programmes designed to address? If the first, they must aim to draw the adult poor back to work. If the second, they must encourage and/or enforce longer working hours among the adult poor. Surely these two problems require very different policy responses and involve different measurements of success. It is unclear to what extent workfare succeeds in addressing either problem—or if any reliable assessment of 'success' is currently possible.

At present the success of workfare programmes is adjudged more in terms of the goals of the state and the workfare agencies than in the terms of the prospects of the individuals engaged in the programmes. It could be argued, then, that any genuine evaluation of the success of workfare programmes would involve far more than reductions in welfare rolls. Rather, it would involve a longer-term tracking of welfare claimants who have undertaken such programmes to assess the 'value-added' of the workfare experience for their earning potential. Much is made in this article of the value of 'self-improvement' in work programmes, but more research needs to be undertaken to establish its long-term consequences for the client, and the extent to which they become more equipped to break down the 'barriers' to work which have shaped their everyday lives.

Workfare and Labour Markets

Workfare marks the spot where welfare, economic and training policies converge. In this respect it has significant implications for all three in terms of both theory and practice. Firstly:

> Workfare amounts to much more than a mean spirited goading of welfare recipients ... Fundamentally, it withdraws universal rights of access to welfare and asserts the primacy of the market as an allocative principle. Workfare represents a thoroughgoing transformation of the institutional bases of the labor market.[9]

and secondly, workfare alerts us to the worrying possibility that:

> training policy and welfare policy are in danger of becoming one and the same.[10]

Workfare therefore marks the site of struggles over economic as well as welfare and educational policy.

Over the past decade, Britain has experienced profound labour market changes which have in many ways paved the way for the workfare experiment. The 1980s signalled a shift to notions of workers 'pricing themselves into jobs', and to increasing labour market flexibility. This has become both a buzz phrase and part of an 'ideological offensive which celebrates pliability and casualisation, and makes them seem inevitable'.[11] But the pitfalls of this 'flexibility' are suffered most by the weakest, who have increasingly found themselves in casual, insecure and low-paid work. But these are precisely the conditions within which US workfare has operated, and which have provided the abundance of jobs which Mead describes as available to the adult poor.

To return briefly to the economic argument central to this article, we need to consider whether US style workfare can (let alone should) be applied in the context of the UK. Mead admits that: 'American work programmes can assume a labour market that generates many available jobs' (p. ix). Notwithstanding the reservations which many hold about what kinds of jobs these actually are, there are still question of whether this can apply to the UK, and so to what extent workfare is appropriate to the conditions of the British labour market. Mead acknowledges that: 'British policy makers will have to ask how far your labour market permits work enforcement—and how far it may be necessary to create jobs' (p. ix). But surely it could be argued that creating jobs would, in any event, be a preferable option and so why not cut out the 'middle-man' [sic] of mandatory workfare?

It is significant that in Wisconsin, cited by Mead as an exemplar of workfare best practice, the success of workfare (in terms of falling welfare caseloads) has been 'driven by administrative muscle and the economy' (p. 46). And so it could be countered that the success of workfare in Wisconsin owes more to the political direction and dynamic economy of the state than to the logic of workfare itself: in other words, if the adult poor were going to find jobs anywhere, it would have been in booming Wisconsin, where workfare could not fail!

Conclusion

Mead's ultimate conclusion is that 'poor adults *must* work much more regularly than they do now' (p. 51). I totally agree with this sentiment, but from a different perspective. I would re-phrase the sentence to read: Poor people *must have the opportunity* to work more regularly than they do now. Although Mead argues that there 'is no alternative' (p. 51), New Labour is currently following the alternative approach of welfare *to* work instead of welfare *for* work. The extent to which this remains distinctive will depend upon several factors:

- the extent of social investment which accompanies the 'New Deals' on offer to the unemployed
- the extent of investment in childcare which accompanies the New Deal for lone mothers
- the success of community partnerships in aiding economic and social regeneration of the poorest localities
- the resources and political will deployed on all of the above!

In the meantime, the first lesson we should learn from Mead's analysis of workfare in America is that it is essential to unravel precisely what we would expect from any workfare experiment in the UK context. Is it to be seen as an attempt to achieve a lasting change in the behaviour and working levels of the adult poor? Or is it to achieve a political 'quick fix' to show that 'something is being done' about welfare dependency, and to reduce the welfare rolls? If it is the former, there is no empirical evidence that workfare will work. If it is the latter, we should not dabble with it as an exercise in deterrence and welfare policing.

Workfare for Lone Mothers:
A Solution to the Wrong Problem?

Melanie Phillips

L AWRENCE MEAD'S analysis rests on the premise that work is the solution to social breakdown. There is no question that both unemployment and the erosion of the work ethic have contributed significantly both to poverty and to other allied social problems. However, the American attachment to the work ethic as the primary means of social and personal transformation has tended to some extent to blur necessary distinctions between discrete social problems. In particular, it appears to permit no discrimination between men and women. Imposing work through workfare is presented as the solution to the welfare dependency of lone mothers. It may end their welfare payments, but that is unlikely to reduce the incidence of lone motherhood or the problems of the children, which it may even exacerbate. It's a solution to the wrong problem.

American commentators tend to view the phenomenon of lone motherhood principally as an unwelcome outcome of the welfare system. This economic determinism is shaped by the fact, particular to the United States, that its main social problem is perceived to be 'welfare mothers'. But lone motherhood is not principally an economic problem and therefore cannot be 'solved' by an economic solution. It is but one element in the far wider cultural phenomenon of family breakdown, a cultural change of great complexity and magnitude. This has arisen not from welfare largesse but from the reduction of the moral universe to the landscape of the unfettered self, a landscape which embraces developments ranging from the denigration of marriage into an ever more meaningless legal concept, through soaring rates of divorce and cohabitation and serial step-parenting to abortion on demand, donor insemination and surrogacy. These related phenomena are being fuelled by a taboo on judgement; by a moral and cultural relativism which prohibits discrimination between lifestyle choices whatever their ill effects; by the separation of sexuality from marriage and procreation and the elevation of sex into *the* supreme lifestyle choice; by the sanctification of the individual's right to make such choices; and by the elevation of personal gratification and the consequent reduction of children to commodities to be disposed of if they get in the way of that gratification. All these factors have contributed to the climate which has produced so many young girls who fall pregnant by young men who then don't want to know them or whom they themselves don't want to know.

Mead's 'solution' does not seek to address any of these factors. It merely deals with welfare, and as a result displays some confusion over precisely what the problem is that it is trying to solve. Is it welfare payments or is it fatherlessness? At the heart of the confusion is a view of men and women as unisex, with identical needs and obligations to work in paid employment. 'Few poor adults work regularly. That is the main reason they are poor', says Mead (p. 1). This may well be true for adult able-bodied men. It is not true, however, for women who are lone mothers. They are not poor because they don't work but because there is no man in the household to earn enough to support the family unit. After all, mothers who are not in paid employment but whose husbands bring in enough income to support the family are not considered to be 'poor'. No-one expects such mothers to work. The idea that lone mothers should be expected to work to support the family unit financially *as well as* care for their children, even when those children are young infants, is a suggestion which once would have been thought preposterous. '[E]mployment failures are the greatest cause of family failures' says Mead (p. 15). In so far as that is true—and it is arguable that there are deeper and more potent causes of family failure—it is the man's unemployment that precipitates the family crisis, not the woman's. It is hardly the case that the traditional family unit with a breadwinning father breaks down because the mother is at home caring for her children. It is probably true that fathers only gain their children's respect if they are employed; it is hardly the case, however, that a child despises its mother for staying home to look after it. Yet Mead lumps both men and women together when he suggests that parental respect depends upon paid employment. This ignores the fact that all successful societies have been built on the principle that mothers are essentially dependent, and should be supported materially and financially (not to mention emotionally and practically) in bringing up their children by the man who has fathered them and thus bears responsibility for the situation he has engendered.

Of course, some mothers want to work and do work full-time from when their children are very young. They are entitled to make that choice. But to expect all lone mothers to do so is either effectively to deny the importance of the maternal caring role, or else to condemn women to a form of servitude in attempting to combine, alone and unsupported, separate roles in conflicting domains. It is expecting them to play the roles of both mother and father, which cannot be in the interests either of the mothers or their children. One might well bemoan the fact that these female-headed families are poor. One might well lament that there is no paid employment bringing in an income to support these families. One might well feel outrage that taxpayers' money is being used to support a lifestyle which is in the interests of neither children nor adults. The long-term welfare dependency of lone mothers *is* a deeply alarming social problem. But none of that means the solution is to force such mothers into the workplace if such a course of action exacerbates the fundamental problem, which is not worklessness but fatherlessness, the harm done to children and the collapse of the male role, identity and socialisation.

And that is precisely the perverse effect that enforced work for lone mothers is likely to produce: the further displacement of thousands of young men from the labour market. This is likely to decrease further the number of marriageable males, young men with sufficient prospects to make them a reasonable proposition for young women. Such a decrease will make lone parenthood more, rather than less, likely. It is surely more important for such young men to work than it is for women who are mothers and already have the responsibility of caring for their children. Paid employment is essential to male identity and role, which are in turn essential to bolting young men into the family unit; which is in turn the main means of socialising and civilising them. Many women want to work, and where they do they should be able to do so. But paid employment is not integral to female identity and role in the way that it is for men.

Yet Mead's argument is a unisex argument. It recognises no difference between women and men, even if those women are mothers. As he has commented, the American public simply doesn't accept the fact that the poor don't work. And more than three quarters of non-poor lone mothers work because, he says, it's thought to be good for the children if the mothers do so.

This claim begs many questions. Working may be better for the mother, but that's not the same as saying it's better for the children. And it's not even clear that it's always in the mother's interests either. Most lone mothers in this country say they want to work but with the crucial caveat 'at some point in the future', not when their children are very young. Evidence shows mothers who work full-time are at least as likely to suffer depression as mothers who don't work.[1] This is hardly surprising, considering the stress of juggling two roles. That stress must increase if the mother is juggling alone and unsupported. Mothers generally want to work part time, increasing their hours as their children grow older. The American view that it is wrong for mothers not to work appears to dismiss the importance and worth of actively caring for their children.

In any event, there's no evidence that Americans think mothers should work, only that mothers on welfare should work. If working motherhood really was so good for children and if it really was so important for a mother's own self-worth, one would expect to see a much wider disapproval of *all* mothers, including those who are married to men who are employed, who choose not to work in paid employment. Clearly, this is not the case. The impetus behind workfare for lone mothers appears to be not that it is wrong for mothers not to work outside the home, but for such mothers to draw welfare. The driving force behind this policy, therefore, is not the wish to further the interests of women or children but outrage at women who depend on state largesse to fund a lifestyle—lone parenthood—of which people disapprove. Its purpose would appear to be punishment for or deterrence against that lifestyle. But the policy not only does nothing to tackle the web of factors behind it; it may even make some of the consequences of that lone parenthood worse for the most vulnerable people in this situation, the children.

Working motherhood has one big drawback. Who looks after the children? Those who advocate this course cannot afford to admit that it may not be in the best interests of the children. And here, welfare conservatives who advocate workfare on the basis that it is a woman's duty to work join forces with unlikely allies, extreme feminists who maintain that women have the 'right' to 'independence' through paid employment regardless of whether or not they are mothers. This group expects the state to pick up the responsibility for childcare to enable mothers to work, and in pursuit of this objective fiercely denies any evidence that substitute childcare may be unsatisfactory for many children, particularly when very young.

Among workfare advocates, the welfare of the children involved does not appears to be taken at all seriously. Mead says: 'Childcare seldom appears to be a serious barrier to employment because it is much cheaper and more available than advocates assert' (p. 8). But in fact it appears that no-one knows whether most children of lone mothers in America who've gone back to work are being cared for by suitable carers; or, indeed, whether they are being cared for by anyone at all.

Mead has said that research shows that children do better if their mothers work. As a generalisation this seems extremely dubious. Some children in certain circumstances may do better. But it is highly unlikely that all children at all ages and regardless of their circumstances do better. It is highly unlikely that pre-school-age children all do better if their mothers work fulltime, considering the large body of mainly American research which, as Patricia Morgan has detailed, shows a range of disadvantages for young children arising from the lack of one-toone interaction in substitute day care, the high proportion of untrained carers and the lack of continuity from frequent changes of staff.[2] Contrary to Mead's assertion, good quality childcare most certainly is not easily available and does not come cheap; it is prohibitively expensive for many families and almost certainly for most lone parents.

The downside of childcare is of course excessively inconvenient for those in both the conservative and extreme feminist camps who think all mothers should work. The feminist camp thinks that, if lone mothers are able to work, this will eradicate their poverty and cement women's independence from men. The conservative camp believes if mothers are made to work this will act as a disincentive to their lone parenthood. But lone mothers are poor not because of the collapse of work but because of the collapse of marriage. Most families now find they cannot make ends meet unless there are one and a half wage packets coming into the household.

The welfare-mother phenomenon cannot be addressed in a vacuum, but only as part of a much wider initiative against the whole phenomenon of family disintegration. Such an initiative might include a promotion and privileging of marriage through both public education and a range of legal and fiscal measures; sharper boundaries in the field of reproductive technology which put the interests of children first; and active encouragement of self-regulation by the media in restoring sexuality to the private domain. Of course, none of this is easy. Reversing cultural slide is a tall order. But there is already enough public unease and anxiety about its more blatant anti-social effects to give such as programme a sporting chance of success. Workfare, by contrast, merely attempts to force *some* women to behave responsibly. Singling these out for social opprobrium means punishing the lowest and most vulnerable for behaviour to which blind eyes are turned among the higher social strata, behaviour which is extolled through the media by privileged citizens from those upper classes.

Enforcement of values through public authority, advocated by Mead, is undoubtedly as necessary as it is controversial. Enforcing the work ethic is desirable for men. But the values to be enforced in addressing the problem of never-married mothers are family values. To say, as Mead does, that workfare was never intended to address the problem of unwed motherhood is surely disingenuous. Such mothers are on welfare because they are unwed. It is the unwed motherhood that the public objects to supporting through taxpayers' money. To say, as Mead does, that although we know how to enforce work we know almost nothing about how to confine pregnancy to marriage is a cop-out. Unlike the Victorian social reformers who dramatically reduced the rate of illegitimacy in the latter part of the nineteenth century, we've never tried. Workfare for lone mothers threatens to punish the poor for having the gall to put into practice the irresponsible hedonism preached at them by the media and ivory-tower intellectuals; while a pusillanimous political class sits on its hands, incapable of doing anything more responsible and courageous than cancelling its cheques.

Rejoinder

Lawrence M. Mead

I AM honoured by the attention British social policy experts have given my work. It is thrilling to discover that my reasonings, developed from afar, have contributed something to what Americans would call the mother of welfare states. In coming over here, I am not carrying coals to Newcastle. At the IEA conference in London where my paper was discussed, I sensed receptivity to its argument, and I did not encounter novel objections. Among the present commentators, several—Field, Grimes, and Philpott—seem to favour of the idea that work should be mandated for the jobless living on benefit, at least in principle. These also seem to be the commentators who know the most about how employment programmes for the disadvantaged actually operate. That is not surprising to me, as most of what I advocate I first heard from programme staff at the local level.

I cannot respond to all the critical points in detail. Here are the main ones, most of them made by more than one commentator, followed by my rebuttals. As in my paper, I use the term 'work-fare' broadly to connote, not only assigning benefit recipients to unpaid jobs, but any policy that requires them to work or do other things promoting employment as a condition of aid.

'Workfare won't work in the UK because barriers to employment are worse here than in the US'

Workfare does assume that jobs are available to recipients required to work. As I admitted in my Foreword, I do not presume that the British labour market generates as many jobs as the American. Some regions are historically depressed, particularly in the North, and it might be necessary to create some jobs there if all the dependent are to work. At the same time, I urge British policy makers not to assume this in advance. The only real test of whether jobs are available is whether people find them when required to. American research and experience

127

suggests that more jobs are available in depressed urban areas, or nearby, than appear to be. The main employment problem the poor have is not in finding work but in keeping it.

John Philpott thinks the restructuring of western economies, which has reduced manufacturing and manual employment, has made many low-skilled men unemployable and may make it impossible to enforce work. This 'mismatch' theory of non-work sounds very plausible, but it has not generated much supportive research in the US. We find that most of our employment is still low- or medium-skilled, and that most of the jobless can find some legal job quickly. Finding a well-paying job is tougher, but even low-paying positions are usually enough to escape poverty and welfare if the parents of families work normal hours. Restructuring is undoubtedly traumatic for many workers, but that struggle does not involve many poor adults, who are seldom steady workers. Few of our long-term poor ever held a factory job. The American labour market, with its static wages but prolific job creation, is tough on the middle class, but it is the best situation for escaping poverty the world has ever seen, as the strong flow of unskilled immigrants to our country attests. As Britain has moved toward a more fluid labour market, the case for lack of jobs weakens.

The notion that disincentives generated by benefits—the 'poverty trap'—explain non-work may be more plausible in Britain than America, because your welfare benefits tend to run higher in relation to earnings than ours do. But again, I have not seen research that really proves this. It is too easy for experts to project their own, optimising mentality on the poor and describe non-work, as Philpott does, as 'a rational economic response' to constraint. If disincentives were important, than we would see a larger response that we do to schemes to improve work incentives such as your Family Credit. When one asks the jobless why they are unemployed, they usually say they are defeated about work, not that working is not worth their while.[1]

'Workfare ignores the structural roots of poverty and inequality'

It is true that in itself workfare promotes social order rather than justice. It requires that the dependent work while leaving the wider structures of the economy and society unquestioned. I do not deny the historic importance of capitalism or the class system—or, in the US, racism—in generating poverty or dependency. We may if we wish attribute social problems entirely to these forces. My argument is the more limited one that it is hard to show a *direct* connection between social conditions and *non-working* poverty in the *present*. After all, in the past society was less fair to the disadvantaged and non-white than it is today, yet work levels then ran higher. Viewed close up, external social circumstances in the US do not explain well why some low-skilled people, such as immigrants, usually work while the dependent poor usually do not. So reforms to promote work on welfare cannot focus on society.

Mostly, the influence of social structure comes via the defeatist attitudes that we call the culture of poverty. People from disadvantaged background often *believe* they are hemmed in by a lack of opportunity so that work is hopeless. But independent inquiry usually finds that work is more possible than people feel. Self-defeat may be understandable given the lives people have lived, but it is seldom a rational response to constraint in the present. The major cause is being raised in families that were too disorganised to inculcate social norms and capacities, often because the parents were themselves jobless and dependent. To say this is not to point blame, because it is precisely through the disabling of the parents—and their parents, and their parents, and so on—that past injustice has its malign influence. But because the immediate roots of non-work usually are not structural, no further social reform in the present, however egalitarian, can overcome it. Even a socialist commonwealth today would have to enforce work. Welfare reform must address non-work as a behaviour, not because it has no social causes, but because the roots are lost in history where they cannot be reached.

Current barriers have much more to do with inequality among the better-functioning mass of the public. Workfare is not an attempt to suppress that issue. To the contrary, nothing would do more to get equality back on the agenda than enforcing work in welfare. Right now, widespread resentment at the lifestyle of long-term benefit recipients blocks any more generous provision for them or other groups that might be deserving. If work is enforced, the recipients become more deserving, and generosity is more popular. With more disadvantaged people in jobs, most of them low-paid, support for unionism and protective labour market reforms would grow. As a conservative, these are costs I accept. The left should be the most, not the least, in favour of work enforcement.

'Workfare blames the victims for problems that are really society's fault'

I am less 'individualist' than critics claim. I do not blame the poor on an individual basis for not working. The causes of prolonged poverty are too mysterious for anyone to be personally to blame for it.[2] If anything, I blame government and the society for refusing to enforce work, especially the élites on left and right who think some new benefit or freedom can solve every social problem.

The poor at present are not responsible for non-work because they do not feel that they are. The defeatism of the culture of poverty means precisely that people do not accept responsibility for themselves. They want to work in principle but feel they cannot in practice. Thus, I reject the brassy psychology assumed by the anti-government right, which pictures the poor as amoral exploiters of the society who would work if only they were denied aid. Would that this were true. In my terms, to say that makes the competence assumption, and it is typically unwarranted.

On the other hand, helplessness does pose serious problems for poor individuals as well as society, so it must be challenged. Nobody who abandons control over his or her life to the environment can command the respect of others. Responsibility cannot be the assumption of policy, but it must be the goal. So I say: the poor must *become* responsible for themselves. That requires that government define the obligations of citizenship to include employment, and to expect the dependent to fulfill them—with some help. That judgment does not involve an individualised finding of fault. It simply applies to the dependent the same expectations as other people face. Government then must create programmes that both help people work and enforce their own effort toward that end. Such programmes are paternalist, combining support services such as childcare with oversight of the clients by case managers—what I call help and hassle.[3] Through them, recipients can become responsible at least for work effort, as is essential to their acceptance by the rest of the society.

Opponents characterise workfare as 'punitive' and predict that it will just make the dependent feel even more helpless. More accurately, it would demoralise competent, middle-class people like themselves. It does not usually demoralise recipients. Surveys done of people put into unpaid jobs shows that they mostly approve the assignment and feel better about being on welfare as a result. Clients whom case managers check up on usually appreciate the attention. The fallacy is to suppose that being obligated is opposed to autonomy. To the contrary, an acceptance of responsibilities, at least about personal conduct, is essential to living a free life. Only people who function can really claim their rights. To be sure, obligation could be overdone or persist too long after families had sorted themselves out, but we are far from that point.

'Workfare aims only to cut the welfare rolls'

I personally deny that reducing dependency is an important goal of reform. Raising work levels among the poor is vastly more significant. Polls show that the public wants to enforce work on welfare adults without ending aid to needy families, and that is exactly what American policy makers are trying to deliver. Last year's federal welfare reform did cut welfare benefits, but mainly outside the lone-parent programmes that are the main object of reform in the US, and most of the cuts were recently restored. Mandatory work policies along with good economic conditions are currently driving welfare caseloads down, saving government money. But meanwhile many states are spending even more on new work programmes and supportive services to move recipients into jobs. The spirit of the reform is surprisingly positive.[4]

It is true that the power of tough work policies to drive people off the rolls or keep them from applying for aid is proving greater than anticipated. Perhaps twice as many people are leaving welfare in the face of work requirements as are going to work, with the others getting support from friends and relatives. But these seem to be the cases who have ready alternatives to welfare. There is little prospect that welfare will be abolished by work-tests, since the fall in the rolls is bound to slow after the more employable cases leave. More likely, states will reprogramme the money they have saved to fund more intensive services to the remaining cases, who are the most troubled.

'Workfare succeeds for other reasons than enforcement'

Several commentators pointed out that I seemed more hard-line in justifying obligation in principle than in describing how workfare really operates. The regime of help and hassle that I recommend can seem little different from what already goes on in top-class voluntary programmes such as the Wise Group, of which Alistair Grimes writes. Perhaps programmes succeed merely because they help people and not because they demand or enforce anything. While effective programmes certainly are well-run and generous, it is going too far to say manditoriness adds nothing. In American experience, voluntary programmes are starved for clients, or they attract only the most motivated—those who would go to work without the help. To reach the more disadvantaged, enforcing participation is indispensable.

'Workfare would undercut voluntary programmes'

The Wise Group is a voluntary programme that has created jobs for the long-term jobless through insulating homes in several locations in Britain. Alistair Grimes fears that it would be inundated by unwilling participants if recipients were forced to enter work programmes. Two rejoinders: First, although the programme appears to be effective, we do not know this; the existing evaluation did not compare outcomes for Wise clients with those for equivalent clients who did not get the programme. Second, there is no reason why Wise should not flourish as a contractor to a mandatory structure where clients were referred to it from benefit programmes. It might well have more clients than it does now, when it must compete with the benefit system. The clients would do less well in absolute terms than the volunteers the programme serves now, but it would probably have more real effect on them.

'Workfare ignores the lone-parent problem'

Melanie Phillips argues that the spread of lone parenthood is the real cause of the welfare problem, and workfare offers no solution to it. I agree that workfare is aimed more at promoting work than solving family problems among the poor. However, Phillips minimises the importance of work to family stability. Failure to provide earnings is the main reason why fathers abandon their families—or are kicked out by their spouses. One aspect of welfare reform is to toughen up child support enforcement. Programmes to require work of fathers owing child support have shown promise in Wisconsin and elsewhere. Some of these programmes try to use child support to re-attach the father to his family.[5]

The difficulty with promoting the family more forcefully is that there is less political mandate to do that than enforce work, and we also know less about how to do it. The truth is that no public policy, however well-funded, has shown much capacity to confine childbearing to marriage. Phillips herself calls for 'a promotion and privileging of marriage through both public education and ... legal and fiscal measures' (p. 125). The very generalities show that she too has little idea about what to do.

Phillips is right that the mother's caring for children has value. In deference to that, I would require her to work only half-time, even if this meant she had to stay partially on welfare. But if the mother is a lone parent, work benefits her child, not only society. American research suggests that the children of lone mothers do better in school if the mothers are employed. Phillips does not believe this research, but she does not cite counter evidence. Nor is childcare the obstacle she believes. Better childcare is of course better for the children than worse, but that is an argument for childcare reform, not against workfare. For welfare mothers to work even with the existing care quality still looks like a gain for families, at least in the US.

Work enforcement does raise issues of fairness and feasibility, yet I find that most of those who raise these concerns are really defending an image of the poor as victims. They say that workfare is too tough, but nothing done to make it more generous causes them to accept any mandatoriness at all. Equally, most of those on the right who oppose welfare refuse to accept that the poor have any special needs or rights, and no evidence to the contrary budges them. These images of identity must be admitted and compromised before welfare reform can proceed. Workfare reflects such a compromise, because it requires *some* responsibility from the poor, while providing them with special help.

Notes

Editor's Introduction

1 Blair MP, Tony, Speech to CPU Conference, Cape Sun Hotel, 14 October 1996.

2 'The 21st Century Welfare State', Social Policy and Economic Performance Conference, Rijksmuseum, Amsterdam, 24 January 1997.

3 In the case of single claimants, the penalty for a first offence will be loss of all benefits for two weeks, and each subsequent refusal will lead to disallowance for a further four weeks. Those with dependants, or who have disabilities, will lose 40 per cent of their benefits for similar periods.

4 *The Observer*, 11 May 1997.

5 Deacon, A., 'Welfare to work: options and issues', in May, M., Brundson, E. and Craig, G. (eds.), *Social Policy Review 9*, Social Policy Association, 1997.

6 Waldfogel, J., 'Ending Welfare As We Know It', *Benefits*, No. 20, October 1997, pp. 11-15; King, D.S., 'The Establishment of Work-Welfare Programs in the United States and Britain', in Steinmo, S., Thelen, K. and Longstreth, F. (eds.), *Structuring Politics*, Cambridge University Press, 1992.

7 Murray, C., *Losing Ground: American Social Policy 1950-1980*, New York: Basic Books, 1984, p. 228.

8 Mead, L.M., *Beyond Entitlement: The Social Obligations of Citizenship*, New York: Free Press, 1986, p. 230.

9 'The Obligation to Work and the Availability of Jobs: A dialogue between Lawrence Mead and William Julius Wilson', *Focus*, Vol. 10, No. 2, 1987, p. 13.

10 Mead, L.M., 'The Hidden Jobs Debate', *Public Interest*, 91, 1988, p. 51.

11 Mead, L.M., *The New Politics of Poverty: The Nonworking Poor in America*, New York: Basic Books, 1992, p. 162.

12 *Ibid.*, p. 238.

13 Mead, L.M., 'The New Politics of the New Poverty', *Public Interest*, 103, 1991, p. 4.

14 Mead, *Beyond Entitlement, op. cit.,*pp. 43, 247.

15 Layard, R. and Philpott, J., *Stopping Unemployment*, London: Employment Policy Institute, 1991.

16 Deacon, A., 'Benefit Sanctions for the Jobless: "Tough Love or Rough Treatment?"', *Economic Report*, Vol. 11, No. 7, London: Employment Policy Institute, July 1997.

From Welfare to Work: Lessons from America

Chapter 1: Poverty and the Failure to Work

1 Much of the following is based on Mead, L.M., *The New Politics of Poverty: The Nonworking Poor in America*, New York: Basic Books, 1992.

2 Sawhill, I.V., 'The underclass: an overview', *The Public Interest*, Vol. 96, Summer 1989, pp. 4-6.

3 Congressional Budget Office, *Trends in Family Income: 1970-1986*, Washington DC: Government Printing Office, 1988, Table A-15.

4 US House of Representatives, Committee on Ways and Means, *1996 Green Book: Background Material, and Data on Programs Within the Jurisdiction of the Committee on Ways and Means*, Washington DC: US Government Printing Office 1996, p. 474.

5 Edin, K. and Jencks, C., 'Reforming welfare', in Jencks, C. (ed.), *Rethinking Social Policy: Pace, Poverty, and the Underclass*, Cambridge MA: Harvard University Press, 1992; Harris, K.M., 'Work and welfare among single mothers in poverty', *American Journal of Sociology*, Vol. 99, No. 2, 1993, 317-52.

6 Edin, K. and Jencks, C., *ibid.*, found that most welfare mothers' unreported income is not from employment, and Harris, K.M., *ibid.*, found that only a minority of mothers have earnings during more than half their time on the rolls. The underground or illegal economy is smaller than many analysts presume, and little of it involves the poor; see Mead, L.M., *The New Politics of Poverty, op. cit.* pp. 52-53.

7 Moffitt, R., 'Incentive effects of the US welfare system: A review', *Journal of Economic Literature* Vol. 30, No. 1, March 1992, pp. 11, 13.

8 Congressional Budget Office, *op. cit.*,1988, Table A-15.

9 US Department of Commerce, Bureau of the Census, *Income, Poverty, and the Valuation of Noncash Benefits: 1993*, Washington DC: Government Printing Office, 1995, Tables D-4, D-5; US Department of Commerce, Bureau of the Census, *Poverty in the United States: 1995*, Washington DC: Government Printing Office, 1996, Table 2.

10 Bane, M.J., 'Household composition and poverty, in Danziger, S.H. and Weinberg, D.H. (eds.), *Fighting Poverty: What Works and What Doesn't*, Cambridge, MA: Harvard University Press, 1986, pp. 226-27.

11 Danziger, S.H. and Gottschalk, P., 'Work, poverty, and the working poor: A multifaceted problem', *Monthly Labor Review*, Vol.109, No. 9, 1986, pp. 17-18.

12 Ellwood, D.T., *Working off of Welfare: Prospects and Policies for Self-sufficiency of Women Heading Families*, Madison: University of Wisconsin, Institute for Research on Poverty, March 1986, pp. 3-5.

Chapter 2: What Stops the Poor from Working?

1 The following is based on Mead, L.M., *The New Politics of Poverty: The Nonworking Poor in America, op. cit.*, chs. 4-6. See also Mead, 'Poverty: How Little We Know', *Social Service Review*, Vol. 68, No. 3, September 1994, pp. 322-50.

2 Bureau of the Census, March 1996, *Current Population Survey*, table 19.

3 'The minimum wage: Its relationship to incomes and poverty', Washington DC: Congressional Budget Office, June 1986, pp. 15-16, 18-19.

4 Burkhauser, R.V. and Finegan, T.A., 'The minimum wage and the poor: the end of a relationship, *Journal of Policy Analysis and Management*, Vol. 8, No. 1, 1989, pp. 59-60.

5 The Harris study uses monthly Panel Study of Income Dynamics (PSID) data. Studies using annual PSID data find a lower proportion of spells ending through employment. Harris, K.M. 'Work and welfare among single mothers in poverty', *op. cit.*, pp. 333-35.

6   Michalopoulos, C. and Garfinkel, I., 'Reducing the welfare dependence and poverty of single mothers by means of earnings and child support: wishful thinking and realistic possibility', Madison: University of Wisconsin, Institute for Research and Poverty, 1989.

7   US House of Representatives, Committee on Ways and Means, *Overview of Entitlement Programs: 1992 Green Book*, Washington DC: Government Printing Office, 1992, p. 1283.

8   Burtless, G., (n.d.), 'The work response to a guaranteed income: A survey of experimental evidence', in Munnel, A.H. (ed.), *Lessons from the Income Maintenance Experiments: Proceedings of a Conference held in September 1986*, Boston: Federal Reserve Bank of Boston, pp. 22-52.

9   Moffitt, R., 'An economic model of welfare stigma', *American Economic Review*, Vol. 73, 1983, p.1033; Moffitt, R., 'Work incentives in transfer programs (revisited): A study of the AFDC program', in Ehrenberg, R.G. (ed.), *Research in Labor Economics*, Vol. 8, Part B, Greenwich, CT: JAI, 1986, pp. 389-439.

10 Turner, M.A., 'Opportunities denied, opportunities diminished: discrimination in hiring', Washington DC: Urban Institute, May 1991.

11 Kirschenman, J. and Neckerman, K.M., 'We'd love to hire them, but...: The meaning of race for employers', in Jencks, C. and Peterson, P.E. (eds.), *The Urban Underclass*, Washington DC: Brookings Institution, 1991, pp. 203-32.

12 Moffitt, R., 'Incentive effects of the US welfare system: a review', *Journal of Economic Literature*, Vol. 30, No. 1, March 1992, pp. 30-31.

13 Blank, R.M., 'The effect of medical need and Medicaid on AFDC participation', *Journal of Human Resources*, Vol. 24, No. 1, 1989, pp. 54-87; Moffitt, R. and Wolfe, B., 'The effect of the medicaid program on welfare participation and labor supply', Madison: University of Wisconsin, Institute for Research on Poverty, January 1990.

14 US Department of Commerce, Bureau of the Census, *Who's Minding the Kids? Childcare Arrangements: Fall 1988*, Series P-70 No. 30, Washington DC: Government Printing Office, 1992, table D; Brush, L.R., 'Childcare used by working women in the AFDC population: an analysis of the SIPP data

base', Paper prepared for the US Department of Health and Human Services, Analysis Research and Training, McLean, VA, 15 October 1987.

15 Unemployment as officially measured, however, is mostly because of the long-term cases. Clark, K.B. and Summers, L.H., 'Labor market dynamics and unemployment: a reconsideration', *Brookings Papers on Economic Activity*, Vol. 1, 1979, pp. 13-72.

16 Freeman, R.B., 'Employment and earnings of disadvantaged young men in a labor shortage economy', in Jencks, C. and Peterson, P.E. (eds.), *The Urban Underclass*, Washington DC: Brookings Institution, 1991, pp. 103-21; Murray, C., 'Here's the bad news on the underclass', *Wall Street Journal*, 8 March 1990, p. A14.

17 Blank, R.M., 'Outlook for the US labor market and prospects for low-wage entry jobs', and Burtless, G., 'Employment prospects of welfare recipients', both in *The Work Alternative: Welfare Reform and the Realities of the Job Market*, Nightingale, D.M. and Haveman, R.H. (eds.), Washington DC: Urban Institute Press, 1995, chs. 3-4.

18 Wilson, W.J., *The Truly Disadvantaged: The Inner City, the Underclass, and Public Policy*, Chicago: University of Chicago Press, 1987; Wilson, W.J., *When Work Disappears: The World of the New Urban Poor*, New York: Knopf, 1996.

19 Borjas, G.J., 'The demographic determinants of the demand for black labor', in Freeman, R.B. and Holzer, H.J. (eds.), *The Black Youth Employment Crisis*, Chicago: University of Chicago Press, 1986, pp. 191-232.

20 Borjas, G.J., Freeman, R.B. and Katz, L.F., 'On the labor market effects of immigration and trade', in Borjas, G.J. and Freeman, R.B. (eds.), *Immigration and the Workforce: Economic Consequences for the United States and Source Areas*, Chicago: University of Chicago Press, 1992, ch. 7.

21 Correlations may be found between economic change and inner-city joblessness, but this does not establish which way the causation runs For an example, see Johnson Jr., J.H., and Oliver, M.A., 'Structural changes in the US economy and black male joblessness: a reassessment', in Peterson, G.J. and Roman, W. (eds.), *Urban Labor Markets and Job Opportunity*, Washington DC: Urban Institute, 1992, ch. 4, pp. 113-47.

22 For a recent reviews of the mismatch literature, see Holzer, Harry J., 'The spatial mismatch hypothesis: what has the evidence shown?' *Urban Studies*, Vol.28, No. 1, February 1991, pp. 105-22; and Holzer, H.J. and Roman, W., 'Mismatches and the urban labor market', in Peterson, G.J. and Vroman, W. (eds.), *op. cit.*, pp. 81-112.

23 Haverman, R.H., *Earnings Inequality: The Influence of Changing Opportunities and Choices*, Washington DC: AEI Press, 1996.

24 Rossi, P.H., *Down and Out in America: The Origins of Homelessness*, Chicago: UnRomanty of Chicago Press, 1989, p. 137.

25 Nasar, S., '90s may be a decade of growth', *New York Times*, 17 February 1993; 'No Need for a Boost', *The Economist*, 13 February 1993, pp. 15-16.

26 US Department of Commerce, Bureau of the Census, *Statistical Abstract of the United States: 1992*, Washington DC: Government Printing Office, 1992, p. 383.

27 Mead, L.M., *The New Politics of Poverty, op. cit.*, ch. 7.

28 Edelman, M.F., *Families in Peril: An Agenda for Social Change*, Cambridge, MA: Harvard University Press, 1987.

29 Lane, R., 'Black Philadelphia, then and now', *The Public Interest*, No. 108, Summer 1992, pp. 35-52. This is the most convincing interpretation of black history that I have read.

30 Tomkins, C., 'A sense of urgency', *New Yorker*, 27 March 1989, pp. 48-74.

Chapter 3: Making Work Pay

1 The following summarises Mead, L.M., *The New Politics of Poverty, op. cit.*, pp. 159-66.

2 Burkhauser, R.V. and Finegan, T.A., *op. cit.*,1989.

3 US House of Representatives, Committee on Ways and Means, *1996 Green Book, op. cit,*, pp. 804-05.

4 Brown, C., Gilroy, C. and Kohen, A., 'The effect of the minimum wage on employment and unemployment', *Journal of Economic Literature*, Vol. 20, No. 2, 1982, pp. 497-99, pp. 505-08; Burtless, G., 'The effect of reform on employment, earnings, and income', in Cottingham, P.H. and Ellwood,

D.T. (eds.), *Welfare Policy for the 1990s*, Cambridge MA: Harvard University Press, 1989, pp. 103-45.

5   Moffitt, R., 'Work incentives in transfer programs (revisited)', *op. cit.* The cuts reduced the proportion of recipients with earnings but only because most of the working recipients were no longer eligible. Incentives may also reduce work levels among low-income workers not on welfare, because they can now more easily qualify for assistance. See Levy, F., 'The labor supply of female household heads, or AFDC work incentives don't work too well', *Journal of Human Resources*, Vol. 14, No. 1, 1979, pp. 76-97.

6   Mead, L.M., *Beyond Entitlement: The Social Obligations of Citizenship*, New York: Free Press, 1986, ch. 11.

7   To maximize its effect, remediation must be aimed at concrete skills needed for particular jobs rather than education for its own sake. See Burghardt, J., Rangarajan, A., Gordon, A. and Kisker, E., *Evaluation of the Minority Female Single Parent Demonstration: Vol. 1, Summary Report*, New York: Rockefeller Foundation, October 1992

8   US House of Representatives, Select Committee on Children, Youth and Families, *A Domestic Priority: Overcoming Family Poverty in America: Hearings Before the Select Committee on Children, Youth and Families*, 100th Cong., 2nd Sess., 22 September 1988, p. 11.

Chapter 4: Radical Solutions from Right and Left

1   Murray, C., *Losing Ground: American Social Policy 1950-1980*, New York: Basic Books, 1984.

2   Technically, TANF is still an entitlement, but only for state governments claiming their funds up to a specified cap, not for individual recipients.

3   National Commission on Children, *Beyond Rhetoric: A New American Agenda for Children and Families*, Washington DC: Government Printing Office, 1991, pp. 94-95.

4   Garfinkel, I., *Assuring Child Support: An Extension of Social Security*, New York: Russell Sage, 1992.

5   Mead, L.M., *Beyond Entitlement, op. cit.*, 1986, ch. 5.

6   The National Commission on Children gave limited attention to the work problem; see, *op. cit.*, 1991, pp. 104-09.

7 According to a simulation reported in Garfinkel, I., Robins, P.K., Wong, P. and Meyer, D.R., 'The Wisconsin child support assurance system: estimated effects on poverty, labor supply, caseloads, and costs', *Journal of Human Resources*, Vol. 25, No. 1, 1990, pp. 16-19, the assured benefit would raise working hours among welfare recipients slightly and might depress them among other workers. It would have little effect on dependency.

In a recent experiment in New York, welfare mothers were offered a child support benefit, somewhat lower than AFDC, in return for much stronger work incentives. This meant they could raise their incomes substantially above AFDC but only if they worked. Only 10 per cent of those eligible took up the offer. See Hamilton, W.L., Burstein, N.R., Hargreaves, M., Moss, D.A. and Walker, M., *The New York State Child Assistance Program: Program Impacts, Costs, and Benefits*, Cambridge, MA: Abt Associates, July 1993.

8 Ellwood, D.T., *Poor Support: Poverty and the American Family*, New York: Basic Books,1988; Ford Foundation Project on Social Welfare, *The Common Good: Social Welfare and the American Future*, New York: Ford Foundation, May 1989; Task Force on Poverty and Welfare, *A New Social Contract: Rethinking the Nature and Purpose of Public Assistance*, Albany: State of New York, December 1986.

9 Kaus, M., *The End of Equality*, New York: Basic Books, 1992, chs. 7-9.

10 DeParle, J., 'Caution on welfare', *New York Times*, 3 February 1993, p. A16; Kramer, M., 'Still waiting for Bill's call', *Time*, Vol. 37, 1 February 1993.

Chapter 5: The Case for Work Requirements

1 Lurie, I., 'A lesson from the JOBS program: Reforming welfare must be both dazzling and dull', *Journal of Policy Analysis and Management*, Vol.15, No. 4, Autumn 1996, pp. 577-78.

2 US General Accounting Office, *Work and Welfare; Current AFDC Work Programs and Implications for Federal Policy*, Washington DC: 1987.

3 Mead, L.M., 'Are welfare employment programs effective?', in Crane, J. (ed.), *Social Programs that Really Work*, New York: Russell Sage Foundation, forthcoming. Figures are

calculated from data on participation levels in the MDRC studies summarised in Table 6.

4 Lynn, Jr, L.E. (ed.), 'Symposium: The craft of public management', *Journal of Policy Analysis and Management*, Vol. 8, No. 2, Spring 1989, pp.284-306.

5 Mead, L.M., 'Expectations and welfare work: WIN in New York City', *Policy Studies Review*, Vol. 2, No. 4, May 1983, pp. 648-62; Mead, L.M., 'Expectations and welfare work: WIN in New York State', *Polity*, Vol. 18, No. 2, Winter 1985, pp. 224-52; Mead, L.M., 'The potential for work enforcement: a study of WIN', *Journal of Policy Analysis and Management*, Vol. 7, No. 2, Winter 1988, pp. 264-88.

   For a parallel analysis in Massachusetts, see Provencher, P.J., 'Welfare recipients and employment: The influence of the attitudes of case managers and other factors on program performance in local welfare offices', PhD thesis, Waltham, MA: Brandeis University, Heller School, August 1989.

6 Hamilton, G., *Interim Report on the Saturation Work Initiative Model in San Diego*, New York: Manpower Demonstration Research Corporation, August 1988, ch. 7. Participation was defined, however, less stringently than under FSA or PRWORA. It could include part-time work or training activities undertaken by the client as well as activities arranged by the programme, and only one hour of activity a month was demanded.

7 Friedlander, D., *Subgroup Impacts and Performance Indicators for Selected Welfare Employment Programs*, New York: Manpower Demonstration Research Corporation, August 1988.

8 Freedman, S. and Friedlander, D., *The JOBS Evaluation: Early Findings on Program Impacts in Three Sites*, New York: Manpower Demonstration Research Corporation, July 1995.

9 Friedlander, D. and Burtless, G., *Five Years After: The Long-Term Effects of Welfare-to-Work Programs*, New York: Russell Sage Foundation, 1995. One reason SWIM's effects faded was that it was dismantled after two years. Its clients could then return to welfare without fear of facing the same régime, as Friedlander and Burtless themselves suggest, p. 146.

10 Riccio, J, Friedlander, D. and Freedman, S., *GAIN: Benefits, Costs, and Three-Year Impacts of a Welfare-to-Work Program*, New York: MDRC, September 1994, pp. 270, 292-93.

11 Friedlander, D. and Burtless, G., *Five Years After, op. cit.*, pp. 78-87, 194-95.

12 Gueron, J.M. and Pauly, E., with Lougy, C.M., *From Welfare to Work*, New York: Russell Sage Foundation, 1991, p. 256; Riccio, J, Friedlander, D. and Freedman, S., *GAIN, op. cit.*, chs., 3, 7.

13 Moffitt, R.A., 'The effect of employment and training programs on entry and exit from the welfare caseload', *Journal of Policy Analysis and Management*, Vol.15, No. 1, Winter 1996, pp. 32-50.

14 The following draws on Mead, L.M., 'The new paternalism in action: welfare reform in Wisconsin', Milwaukee: Wisconsin Policy Research Institute, March 1996. Much of that analysis was published in Mead, L.M., 'Optimizing JOBS: evaluation versus administration', *Public Administration Review*, Vol. 57, No. 2, March/April 1997, pp. 113-23.

15 The statistical analyses, reported in Mead, L.M., 'The decline of welfare in Wisconsin', Milwaukee: Wisconsin Policy Research Institute, March 1996, pp. 17-22, include a time series of the statewide caseload trend and three cross-sectional analyses of caseload decline across the 72 Wisconsin counties. For a parallel analysis with similar conclusions, see Wiseman, M., 'State strategies for welfare reform: The Wisconsin story', *Journal of Policy Analysis and Management*, Vol. 15, No. 4, Autumn 1966, pp. 515-46.

For comparable analyses in other states, see Schiller, B.R. and Brasher, C.N., 'Workfare in the 1980s: Successes and limits', *Policy Studies Review*, Vol. 9, No. 4, Summer 1990, pp. 665-80; Englander, V. and Englander, F., 'Workfare in New Jersey: A five year assessment', *Policy Studies Review*, Vol. 5, No. 1, August 1985, pp. 33-41; Brasher, C.N., 'Workfare in Ohio: Political and socioeconomic climate and program impact', *Policy Studies Journal*, Vol. 22, No. 3, Autumn 1994, pp. 514-27.

16 Calculated from monthly caseload data from the Wisconsin Department of Health and Social Services.

Chapter 6: The Future of Work Enforcement

1 Hagen, J.L. and Lurie, I., *Implementing JOBS: Progress and Promise*, Albany: State University of New York at Albany, Rockefeller Institute of Government, August 1994.

2　As noted above, SWIM achieved 52 per cent on a monthly basis, but only if a wide range of activities were included, and participation required only one day of activity a month. Kenosha, Wisconsin achieved over 60 per cent by this measure and 50 per cent by the measure used in JOBS. See Wiseman, M., 'Sample Family Support Act Job Opportunity and Basic Skills Training (JOBS) Participation Data (Revised)', Madison: University of Wisconsin—Madison, La Follette Institute of Public Affairs, November 24, 1991.

3　I refer here to my own and others' studies of welfare/work programmes using sub-units as the units of analysis and employing statistical controls to adjust for non-programme influences. The methodology controls for these factors less surely than experimental evaluations but reveals much more about how programmes work. For a defense, see Mead, L.M., 'Welfare policy: the administrative frontier', *Journal of Policy Analysis and Management*, Vol. 15, No. 4, Autumn 1996, pp. 587-600.

4　This view is shared by most but not all case workers in these programmes. See US General Accounting Office, *Work and Welfare: Analysis of AFDC Employment Programs in Four States*, Washington DC: US Government Printing Office, January 1988, pp. 34-37.

5　Friedlander, D. and Burtless, G., *Five Years After, op. cit.*, pp. 27, 33, 77, 87, 149.

6　Mead, L.M., 'The new paternalism in action', pp. 21, 30; Mead, L.M., 'Expectations and welfare work: WIN in New York City', *Policy Studies Review*, Vol. 2, No. 4, May 1983, p. 659; Mead, L.M., 'Expectations and welfare work: WIN in New York State', *Polity*, Vol. 18, No. 2, Winter 1985, pp. 237-38. At the state level, however, sanctioning is positively linked to performance, probably because it is linked to overall implementation levels; see Mead, L.M., 'Potential for work enforcement,' pp. 271-73.

7　Mead, L.M.,'Optimizing JOBS', pp. 118-19.

8　Mead, L.M.,'Optimizing JOBS', p.119.

9　Mead, L.M., 'Optimizing JOBS,' pp. 119-21.

10 Mead, L.M., 'Decline of welfare', pp. 19-23. Again, there are some other statistical analyses to the same effect. See Schiller, B.R. and Brasher, C.N., 'Workfare in the 1980s', *op.*

cit.; Englander, V. and Englander, F., 'Workfare in New Jersey, *op. cit.*; Brasher, C.N., 'Workfare in Ohio', *op. cit.*

11 Hagan, J.L. and Lurie, I., *Implementing JOBS: Case-management Services*, Albany: State University of New York at Albany, Rockefeller Institute of Government, July 1994.

12 Bardach, E., *Improving the Productivity of JOBS Programs*, New York: Manpower Demonstration Research Corporation, December 1993, p. 19.

13 Chadwin, M.L., Mitchell, J.J. and Nightingale, D.S., 'Reforming welfare: Lessons from the WIN experience', *Public Administration Review*, Vol. 41, No. 3, May/June 1981, pp. 375-76.

14 Maslach, C., 'Burned-out', *Human Relations*, Vol. 5, No. 9, September 1976, pp. 16-22.

15 Goodwin, L., *Do the Poor Want to Work? A Social-Psychological Study of Work Orientations*, Washington DC: Brookings Institution, 1972.

16 Gueron, J.M. and Pauly, E., with Lougy, C.M., *From Welfare to Work, op. cit.*, p. 166, summarises these results. For more detail, see Brock, T., Butler, D. and Long, D., 'Unpaid work experience for welfare recipients: Findings and lessons from MDRC research', New York: MDRC, September 1993, table 5. The one instance where a majority was dissatisfied to be working for benefits was in Chicago.

17 Foderaro, L.W., 'Leaving welfare behind by degrees', *New York Times*, September 16 1990, p. 38.

18 Bardach, E., *Improving the Productivity of JOBS Programs, op. cit.*, pp.18-19.

19 A question raised by students of 'street-level' bureaucracy is how far one can believe what welfare managers say about programme operations. Perhaps welfare administration is more punitive in practice than in its professed policies. See Lipsky, M., 'Bureaucratic disentitlement in social welfare programs', *Social Service Review*, Vol. 58, No. 1, March 1984, pp. 3-27. One solution I use to that problem is to interview confidentially at all levels of programmes; I generally find what executives say consistent with what line-level staff say. Another is to check what administrators say against how clients are actually assigned as indicated by programme reporting data.

Chapter 7: An Assessment of Work Enforcement

1 Mead, L.M., *Beyond Entitlement, op. cit.*, pp. 233-40; Mead, L.M., *The New Politics of Poverty, op. cit.*, pp. 57-63.

2 Schorr, L.B. with Schorr, D., *Within our Reach: Breaking the Cycle of Disadvantage*, New York: Doubleday, 1988.

3 Mead, L.M., 'The new paternalism in action', *op. cit.*, pp. 34-36.

4 Plotnick, R.D., 'Welfare and out-of-wedlock childbearing: evidence from the 1980s', *Journal of Marriage and the Family*, Vol. 52, No. 3, August 1990, pp. 735-46.

5 Mead, L.M., *Beyond Entitlement, op. cit.*, chs. 8-11.

6 Bane, M.J. and Ellwood, D., *Welfare Realities: From Rhetoric to Reform*, Cambridge, MA: Harvard University Press, 1994, ch. 1.

7 For several case studies of states, see Norris, D.F. and Thompson, L. (eds.), *The Politics of Welfare Reform*, Thousand Oaks, CA: Sage, 1995; and Nathan, R.P., *Turning Promises into Performance: The Management Challenge of Implementing Workfare*, New York: Columbia University Press, 1993.

8 Hamilton, G, *Interim Report on the Saturation Work Initiative Model in San Diego*, New York: Manpower Demonstration Research Corporation, August 1988, pp. 15-17.

9 Corbett, T.J., 'Welfare reform in Wisconsin: The rhetoric and the reality', in Norris D.F. and Thomson, L. (eds.), *The Politics of Welfare Reform, op. cit.*, ch. 2; Peterson, P.E. and Rom, M.C., *Welfare Magnets: A New Case for a National Standard*, Washington, DC: Brookings Institution, 1990, ch. 2.

10 Heclo, H., 'Poverty politics', in Danziger, S.H., Sandefur, G.D. and Weinberg, D.H. (eds.), *Confronting Poverty: Prescriptions for Change*, New York: Russell Sage Foundation, and Cambridge, MA: Harvard University Press, 1994, ch. 15.

11 Mead, L.M., 'Decline of Welfare', *op. cit.*, pp. 27-29.

Chapter 8: The Political Dimension of Workfare

1 Mead, L.M., *Beyond Entitlement, op. cit.*, chs. 3-5; Mead, L.M., *The New Politics of Poverty, op. cit.*, ch. 9.

2 Mead, L.M., *The New Politics of Poverty, op. cit.*, pp. 57-61.

3   Mead, L.M., *Beyond Entitlement, op. cit.*, chs. 8-9.

4   Mead, L.M., *The New Politics of Poverty, op. cit.*, ch. 9.

5   Ellwood, D.T., 'Welfare reform as I knew it: when bad things happen to good policies', *The American Prospect*, No. 26, May-June 1996, pp. 22-29.

6   Brown, P., *Minority Party: Why Democrats Face Defeat in 1992 and Beyond*, Washington DC: Regnery Gateway 1991; Edsall, T.B. and Edsall, M.D., *Chain Reaction: The Impact of Race, Rights, and Taxes on American Politics*, New York: Norton, 1991; Mead, L.M., *The New Politics of Poverty, op. cit.*

Commentaries

Re-inventing Welfare: A Response to Lawrence Mead

1   Gregg, P. and Wadsworth, J., *Economic Report*, Vol. 10, No. 3, London: Employment Policy Institute, March 1996.

2   White, M., *The Welfare-to-Work Report*, York: The Joseph Rowntree Foundation, September 1997.

Lessons From America: Workfare and Labour's New Deal

1   'The Will to Win', Speech by the Prime Minister, the Right Hon. Tony Blair MP, at the Aylesbury Estate, Southwark, Monday 2 June, 1997.

2   See the Employment Policy Institute's quarterly *Employment Audit*. Most of the statistics cited in this commentary are drawn from the Audit which is based on official statistics.

3   *Ibid.*

4   Business Strategies Ltd., *Occupations for the Future*, 1996.

5   *Employment Audit, op. cit.*

6   *Ibid.*

7   *Ibid.*

8   Layard, R., *What Labour Can Do*, London: Warner Books, 1997.

9   OECD, *The Jobs Study*, 1994; Layard, R. and Philpott, J., *Stopping Unemployment*, London: Employment Policy Institute, 1991.

10 For a discussion of the compulsion issue and opposing views see Deacon, A., 'Benefit Sanctions for the Jobless: "Tough Love or Rough Treatment?"', *Economic Report*, Vol. 11, No. 7, London: Employment Policy Institute, July 1997.

Workfare—a Pull, a Push or a Shove?

1 Beck, U., *Risk Society: Towards a New Modernity*, London: Sage, 1993, p. 49.

2 Giddens, A., *Modernity and Self-Identity: Self and Society in the Later Modern Age*, Cambridge: Polity Press, 1991.

3 Beck., U., *op. cit.*

4 *Ibid.*, p. 89.

5 There is insufficient space here to discuss whether the UK treatment of lone parents as exempt from work requirements is right or wrong.

6 Beck,U., *op. cit.*, p. 136.

7 Sheehan, M. and Tomlinson, M., 'Long-term unemployment in West Belfast', in McLaughlin, E. and Quirk, P. (eds.), *Policy Aspects of Employment Equality in Northern Ireland*, Belfast: The Standing Advisory Commission on Human Rights, 1996.

8 Katz, M., *The Underclass Debate: Views from History*, Princeton: Princeton University Press, 1993.

9 McLaughlin, E. 'Researching the Behavioural Effects of Welfare Systems', in Bradshaw, J. and Millar, J. (eds.), *Social Welfare Systems: Towards a Research Agenda*, Bath: ESRC/University of Bath Social Policy Papers No. 24, 1996.

10 Wilkinson, R., 'Health, Redistribution and Growth', in Glyn, A. and Miliband, D. (eds.), *Paying for Inequality: the Economic Cost of Social Injustice*, London: Rivers Oram Press, 1994.

11 Doyal, L. and Gough, I., *A Theory of Human Need*, London: Macmillan, 1991.

12 *Ibid.*, pp. 59-60.

13 Sen, A., *Inequality Re-examined*, Oxford: Clarendon, 1992.

14 Weale, A., *Political Theory and Social Policy*, London: Macmillan, 1983.

15 Sen, *op. cit.*

16 See Fryer, D., 'Psychological or material deprivation: why does unemployment have mental health consequences?', in McLaughlin, E. (ed.), *Understanding Unemployment: New Perspectives on Active Labour Market Policies*, London: Routledge, 1992.

17 Doyle and Gough, *op. cit.*

18 Beck, *op. cit.*, p. 135.

19 *Ibid.*, p. 131.

20 *Ibid.*, p. 135.

21 *Ibid.*

22 *Ibid.*

23 Lash, S. and Wynne, B. 'Introduction' to Beck, U., *Risk Society: Towards a New Modernity*, London: Sage, 1992, p. 5.

24 *Ibid.*, pp. 7-8.

Would Workfare Work? An Alternative Approach for the UK

1 This does not mean that I subscribe, in general, to the culture-of-poverty hypothesis.

2 McGregor, A., Ferguson, Z., Fitzpatrick, J., McConnachie, M. and Richmond, K., *Bridging the Jobs Gap: An Evaluation of the Wise Group and the Intermediate Labour Market*, York: The Joseph Rowntree Foundation, 1997.

3 Hirst, A., *Glasgow Works Evaluation: The Final Report*, Glasgow Development Agency, 1996.

From Welfare to Work—and Back Again?

1 Cook, D., *Rich Law, Poor Law*, Milton Keynes: Open University Press, 1989, p. 63.

2 Oppenheim, C. and Harker, L., *Poverty: The Facts*, London: Child Poverty Action Group, 1996.

3 *Journal of Social Policy*, Vol. 26, No. 3, 1997, p. 383.

4 Murray, C., *The Emerging British Underclass*, London: IEA Health and Welfare Unit, 1990.

5 Cook, D., *Poverty, Crime and Punishment*, London: Child Poverty Action Group, 1997.

6 'The Will to Win', Speech by the Prime Minister, the Right Hon. Tony Blair MP, at the Aylesbury Estate, Southwark, 2 June, 1997; Harman MP, H., Secretary of State for Social Security, DSS Press Release, 2 June 1997.

7 Foucault, M., *Discipline and Punish*, Harmondsworth: Penguin, 1977.

8 Christie, N., *Crime Control as Industry*, London: Routledge, 1993.

9 Peck, J., *Work Place: The Social Regulation of Labor Markets*, New York: Guildford Press, 1996, p.187.

10 *Ibid.*, p. 185.

11 Pollert, 1988, quoted in Peck, *op. cit.*, p. 137.

Workfare for Lone Mothers: A Solution to the Wrong Problem?

1 Morgan, P., *Who Needs Parents?, The Effects of Childcare and Early Education on Children in Britain and the USA*, London: IEA Health and Welfare Unit, 1996, Chapter 10, 'Mothers Go Mad'.

2 Morgan, P. *op. cit.*

Rejoinder from Lawrence Mead

1 I address these barriers and labour market issues more fully in my book *The New Politics of Poverty: The Nonworking Poor in America*, New York: Basic Books, 1992, Chapters, 4-6.

2 Mead, L.M., 'Poverty: How Little We Know', *Social Service Review*, Vol. 68, No. 3, September 1994, pp. 322-50.

3 See Mead, L.M. (ed.), *The New Paternalism: Supervisory Approaches to Poverty*, Washington DC: Brookings Institution, 1997.

4 DeParle, J., 'US Welfare System Dies As State Programs Emerge', *New York Times*, 30 June 1997, pp. A1, B8.

5 Mincy, R.B. and Pouncy, H., 'Paternalism, Child Support Enforcement and Fragile Families', in Mead, L.M. (ed.), *The New Paternalism, op. cit.*

Index